Writing the Nonfiction Book

Every topic, every page, of Eva Shaw's *Writing the Nonfiction Book* is information dense. If you're standing in a bookstore reading this and thinking you will get enough of her sound advice with a quick browse, you'll be sorry. Buy the book. It's a small investment in your dream of writing a book.

Jack Canfield, CEO
Chicken Soup for the Soul Enterprises, Inc.
www.chickensoup.com

As you read through *Writing the Nonfiction Book*, Eva will move into your writing life and become your mentor. You'll sense that she is sitting next to you, coaching you on, should you ever get tired or muddled or begin to doubt that you have what it takes. Her words, straight from these pages, will come back to you as you stare at that computer screen or your pencil and paper, and suddenly the process will make sense.

Dan Poynter, Author, Publisher, Speaker
The Self-Publishing Manual
http://www.ParaPublishing.com

Eva Shaw reveals elusive publishing secrets. She provides a comprehensive, practical guide, jam-packed with fun extras. This woman knows her stuff and is willing to divulge all. If you've ever thought about writing a nonfiction book, the first step is to read this one.

Debbie Macomber, Bestselling Romance Novelist
Mira Publishing

Let Eva Shaw and *Writing the Nonfiction Book* propel you into the world of published writers. I highly recommend this book. Read it thoroughly, whether you're just considering how you fit into a writing future or if you have been writing for years. Eva's sparkling enthusiasm for writing spills onto every page of this essential volume for the soon-to-be-published book writer.

Celeste Mergens, Conference Director
Whidbey Island Writers Conference

Reading this book is like inviting a friendly, insightful teacher over to your place – that place where you've said, "Someday I'll write a book." Count on the best advice, and count on it being right if you get it from Eva Shaw. She was on target in her previous book, *The Successful Writer's Guide to Publishing Magazine Articles*, and once more she's there for writers with *Writing the Nonfiction Book*.

Pat Bell, Author, Publisher
Cat's Paw Press

Eva Shaw simplifies producing and marketing the nonfiction book into workable steps to help any writer stay on track. She demystifies the entire process, converting it into a practical, no-nonsense approach that leads you all the way through your nonfiction book project. Eva's enthusiasm for writing shines on every page.

Donna Marganella
Essayist, Humor Writer

Do you have the desire and determination to become a published writer? I guarantee that if you follow Eva Shaw's tricks of the trade, you will be successful. These are the tricks she used to become a fulltime writer, admired college instructor, and sought-after conference speaker.

Cheryl Allred, Teacher, Artist, Writer

Eva Shaw knows how to sell books. A successful writer and teacher, Eva presents her methods in an easy-to-read and easy-to-follow format. As a university professor, writer, and teacher of writing courses, I have followed her advice, and her career, for many years. Most of us write for pleasure or to satisfy a need, but we don't make a living with our words. Eva does. Her methods, presented as if she were sitting with you over a cup of coffee and describing how to write and sell your book, work! If anyone can help you get your book finished and sold, Eva Shaw can do it. Enjoy the ride.

Diane M. Yerkes, Ed.D., Professor of Education
San Diego State University, San Diego

If I had to sum up Eva Shaw in one word, it would be *enthusiasm*. She eagerly shares her passion for writing with others and her love of the written word shows in everything she says and does. As a former student, I can honestly say that I have benefited from her energized lessons. She has a way of teaching writers to tap into their inner creativity.

Charlene S. Engeron, Novelist and Newspaper Reporter

When Eva Shaw edited my first attempts to write, she miraculously made me feel as if I had succeeded in a major accomplishment. Her suggestions were of immeasurable value to me, but most of all, she gave me a shot in the arm that kept me going. I'll always be grateful for her wise and appropriate remarks. What a gift!

Dr. Herb Neufeld, Retired Principal
Shafter High School, Shafter, California

I am so grateful *Writing the Nonfiction Book* found its way to me. This powerful book teaches the nuances of nonfiction writing. It has usable tools that are simple and effective. Eva Shaw once again exposes us to the real world of writing. It is the next best thing to having Eva as your personal (writing) trainer. I highly recommend this book.

C. J. Johnson, M.A.
Psychotherapist, Writer

It's easy to get lost on the journey to writing a nonfiction book unless you hit the trail with an experienced guide. Eva Shaw, author of scores of nonfiction books and a natural-born teacher, is more than an experienced guide, she's a regular Eagle Scout. She can help you navigate through the brush and make it to your journey's end — a published book.

Paul S. Levine, Esq.
Literary Agent and Entertainment Law Attorney
Venice, California

Writing the Nonfiction Book

A Successful Writer's Guide

Eva Shaw, Ph.D.

Rodgers & Nelsen
Publishing Co.
Loveland, Colorado

ISBN 0-9662696-2-4

First Edition 1999

Printed in the United States of America

Writing the Nonfiction Book is published by:

Rodgers & Nelsen Publishing Co.
P.O. Box 7001
Loveland, CO 80537-0001
970/593-9557

Production Credits:

Edited by Bobette W. Host
Cover, Layout, and Production by VW Design

Library of Congress Cataloging-in-Publication Data

Shaw, Eva, 1947–
    Writing the nonfiction book: a successful writer's guide / by Eva Shaw.
        p.   cm.
    Includes bibliographical references (p.) and index.
    ISBN 0-9662696-2-4 (trade pbk.)
    1. Authorship.   I. Title.
PN145.S46   1999
808' .02--dc21   99-36355
                                                                          CIP

Dedicated

To every writer with a book waiting to be written.

And to Zippy.

How to Get the Most from This Book

This book has wide margins for a reason. *Writing the Nonfiction Book* is meant to be *used* – make notes in it, scribble a thought, use a highlighter, carry it in your backpack, dog-ear the pages, take it to lunch, make it part of your daily life. Just *use* it.

This is your practical guide to becoming a successful writer of nonfiction books. Fill the book with your personal additions to the text for your own reference. You don't need a plug-in to use this "laptop." You can open it up anytime and anywhere.

Read, make notes, and gain further insight. Then convert it all to queries, proposals, and sales!

Contents

Acknowledgments

All books have beginnings — that spark that connects one brain cell to another, and suddenly the mind says, "Hey, that's good."

This book's spark did a zillion laps around my brain until Craig Nelsen, genius publisher, validated that I should put in the time and effort to write it. Craig listened to my ideas and let me ponder what should and shouldn't be included within these pages. He also knew that, like a superb soup, a book has to simmer to get the right flavors you'll find in these pages.

Joe Shaw, my husband, continues to be my most loved and biggest fan and my best marketing tool. When we attend writers' conferences together, he is the first to tell writers about this book. He knows it inside and out and believes every writer on the planet needs a copy in hand. Now that's love and dedication and salesmanship.

Thank you, most of all, to my students, seminar attendees, conference audiences, and fellow writers who have been the cheering section and inspiration for this book.

Remember: Just write.

Foreword

Nine out of ten of us have a book inside that is ready to be written. No matter how we try to shake off those feelings, the ideas stay put. If you fit into this picture, listen up.

I've been in the publishing business for thirty years. I found out early on that the physical act of book writing bogs down most writers. Maybe you've been struggling with this too? Just how do we get from Point A (a dynamite idea) to Point Z (getting the book ready for self-publication or presentation to a publisher)?

Then there's the motivation that it takes. Writing can be lonely and make us feel alienated and even creatively blocked. How can we avoid this? How can we stay focused when concepts sometimes scatter like so much dust in the wind? How in the world is it possible to predict what readers will want in the future? Then there are the practical issues. How can we secure a great interview with no track record in publishing? How can we research and make every moment count? How can we gain credibility in print while writing or promoting our book?

Eva Shaw gives you the answers to these puzzles in her *Writing the Nonfiction Book.*

When Eva and I first talked about this book and the need for a concise, easy-to-read manual on book writing, I remember saying, "It's about time I have a book I can recommend."

When I speak and write about self-publishing, I take writers through the writing process. Yet, I have always known that to start a book, you need more than a viable idea. You have to acquire the writing smarts to "pull it off."

Some writing teachers just tell folks who have a book in their hearts or heads to, "Forget about format, marketability, and concepts – it will come together." Ah, if it were only that easy. But writing a book isn't like sitting down to balance your checking account or figure out new software. Writing a book takes planning and it helps if you have clear guidelines – or a recipe.

Actually writing a book is a lot like cooking the perfect Thanksgiving meal. It requires more preparation than you can imagine, especially if you have never done it before. In writing a book and cooking a turkey, there is plenty that can go wrong, too. Just ask anyone who's burned that bird. With experience, you learn to maneuver through the entire adventure and create the consummate feast. First-timers often struggle to make the end result as desirable as they had hoped.

It used to be the same for those who had not gone through the book-writing process. Now Eva has created a way to make the experience satisfying and sensational — just like eating a delicious Thanksgiving dinner. So if you want to think of *Writing the Nonfiction Book* as your recipe to book-writing success, I'll agree to that. And hand me the mashed potatoes and gravy and I'll get you going in self-publishing if that's the direction you choose.

Seriously, I've examined shelves full of writing books and this book of Eva's is the most complete plan for writing a nonfiction book you'll find anywhere. With it, you'll get Eva Shaw.

As you read through *Writing the Nonfiction Book*, Eva will move into your writing life and become your mentor. You'll sense that she is sitting next to you, coaching you on should you ever get tired or muddled, or begin to doubt that you have what it takes. Her words, straight from these pages, will come back to you as you stare at that computer screen or your pencil and paper, and suddenly the process will make sense.

As your literary coach, she'll help you express your ideas so that they come alive. Of course, she will make you do the work, yet she will tell you how to streamline the process. Sure she might ask you to sweat over a phrase, cross out an entire chapter, or rewrite your entire book, but you'll find her reassurance steadfast. You can do it.

"Publishing is hard work." I've made that declaration to at least a million people during my seminars and in every one of the eleven editions of *The Self-Publishing Manual.* Writing is labor-intensive, too, but the gratification of sharing your knowledge, your heart, and your soul make it all worthwhile.

Like a fine mentor and an inspirational coach, Eva gives you the big picture and then turns you loose to write, checking in with helpful information along the way. As I've done in the publishing industry, Eva walks you through the writing process with simple, clear, understandable steps. And, great news for every writer, she writes in plain English.

If you're the one person out of those nine people who really has a book to write, the book you're holding now is the answer. And once you get that first book under your belt, the next is a whole lot easier. Just ask Eva — she's written more than forty. Just ask me. I've written twenty-nine, plus sixty revisions, and I'm still going strong.

Dan Poynter
The Self-Publishing Manual
www.ParaPublishing.com

Introduction

Have you ever thought of how you would feel seeing your words in a book? Do you love to write and dream of being a writer? Could you draft just one page a day? Do you enjoy nonfiction? If you've been nodding your head, then you have what it takes to write a nonfiction book.

There's money to be made writing nonfiction books. There's also celebrity status in being a writer. And there's incredible satisfaction seeing your book on the bookstore shelf and in the hands of readers.

Writing a book is practically a national wish. Ask ten people if they've ever thought about it, and you'll most likely get nine who say, "Yes." That tenth one is probably thinking, "Well, sometimes."

Of course, there are scores of would-be writers who fantasize about some day penning *The Great American Novel*. Writing fiction is the stuff that dreams are made of, with dashing heroes and delicious heroines, daring plots and captivating conspiracies that are as convoluted as the mind can imagine.

Fiction is fun to write, but fiction isn't everyone's cup of tea. It's not mine, nor is it right for thousands of other nonfiction book writers. Like you, we're interested in writing nonfiction *and* making money. We write on topics that are as real as today's headlines. We write the books publishers buy and people read.

Fiction writers take note: If you currently write fiction and haven't sold any of your work yet, writing and selling a non-fiction book could help you get your tootsie in the door. Sure, selling a nonfiction book before a novel may be getting to the success you've imagined through the back door, but when you're at the top, will that matter? Even if you're determined to stick to fiction, use the methods in this book to break into the publishing world and use the success tips to launch your novel.

If you've ever wondered if you could write a book, the answer is, yes, you can. This book tells everything you need to know to successfully write a nonfiction book geared to the adult and older teenage reader. The information is also applicable if you're writing nonfiction for the young reader, because the points we cover relate to that book consumer too.

This guide tells more than just how to write your book. It tells how to sell and promote your book. The system works. I know from firsthand experience.

Every year more than 50,000 books are published in the United States, and 75 percent are nonfiction books. They come from writers just like you. It's a good thing we're prolific because Americans can't get enough of nonfiction. For the first time, here's a book that takes you from *initial idea* to the *final book*.

You can write a book. Yes, that book inside you can come out and you can see your words in print.

This book will get you to write and publish nonfiction. It includes the vital steps for determining an idea's marketability and targeting a reading audience. It describes popular book topics, gives step-by-step instruction for writing, and shows you how to format a manuscript, along with nearly painless tips for self-editing. You'll also get a crash course on how to find an agent and book publisher and how to get extra publicity even after the book has been out for years.

I write commercial nonfiction books — more than forty since I quit my day job to become a fulltime writer. I write books Americans buy and read. However, in the 1980s, when I first decided writing was my life, I floundered. It wasn't easy, and I took some wrong turns.

I'm a logical person. I wanted steps, not some wishy-washy hype found in many writing magazines. Yet that's all I discovered "out there," and as all writers worth their salt know, it's nearly impossible to type with one's fingers crossed. Wishes are great, but you have to work hard to see them transformed into reality.

You might have already discovered, as I did, that creative writing classes don't help launch nonfiction book-writing careers. Please don't misunderstand. Creative writing classes are important places for beginning writers to learn technique and gain confidence. However, because I didn't want to write poetry, prose, or a novel, the classes often left me even more confused. All too often creative writing classes are taught by people with little real nonfiction writing and publishing experience. I had been in the business world too long to accept information from people who had less experience than I did. Even in some of the university classes, the skill level of the instructor standing behind the podium was less than what I expected or needed. If you've been down this highway, please know I share your frustration.

In my search for how to write and sell a nonfiction book, I realized that I needed a plan. I wanted to know the how-tos without the baloney, so I created my own methods and found they worked. I felt like a gourmet chef as I attempted to create the best of the best, taking a pinch of this and a dash of that and frequently ignoring criticism and rejection. Along the way, I threw out some popular but antiquated advice, and discovered plenty of short cuts. The result is a nearly mistake-proof method on how to write and sell a nonfiction book.

This is the book I wished for in the beginning. Now it's here for you. It's designed around the material I present at universities and conferences throughout the country. Twenty years of my experience are rolled up into these pages. Everything is clear, sequential, and true.

Although some well-meaning authors would tell you quite differently, there are no secrets to writing the nonfiction book. Throughout this book, the tricks of the trade are identified by the icon at various points in the book. If you need a quick jolt of motivation or writing reality, skim through and read a few of them right now. Here's what to look for:

 ## Get Started Now

The concepts you'll find within these pages work. They're short, sweet, and snappy because who among us has time for a lengthy volume of literary wisdom?

If you have enough time to pour over a verbose dissertation on writing, there are plenty of lengthy books at the library. And if you don't want to find better ways to work, you're probably independently wealthy and writing is a hobby. That's okay. Gently pass this book on to a writer who needs it and wants to make a living.

Participants in my university classes and conference programs do *Creative Aerobics*. These are exercises to boost and sharpen the creative process. In my classes, students start and finish each session with a Creative Aerobic exercise. Just like the muscles we use in physical aerobic exercises, the more our creative muscles are used, the stronger they become. I urge writers of all levels and genres to write every day. If you need to flex your creative muscles right now, look for the Creative Aerobic icon at the end of any chapter and get hopping.

The methods presented here to write a nonfiction book are analytical and orderly. The approach is highly creative. It's fun. Why settle for less? As you use the system and modify it to your needs, you'll be able to brainstorm and break ideas down into workable chunks, whether you're writing or promoting your book. These smaller pieces allow you to manage even a gigantic book project with ease and the savvy of the seasoned pro.

Sound simple? It is.

CHAPTER 1

From Idea to Bestseller

A book is like a garden
carried in the pocket.
— *Chinese Proverb*

"There's a book in me."

"I really want to write a book."

"If only I knew how to put my thoughts down, I'm sure I could write a bestseller."

How often have you heard these words? At writing conferences, while chatting with new friends and during writing classes I teach at a nearby university, I hear these sentences a lot, often on a daily basis.

If the truth be known, most of us dream of putting ideas to paper, creating a book, fulfilling aspirations of authorship. Without assistance, and even with the best intentions, the majority fail. But it doesn't have to be that way. With a solid, sensible writing plan — a road map — you can become a book writer. You can be a published author.

That's what *Writing the Nonfiction Book* is all about. So if you're a determined writer, regardless of your writing or publishing experience, you can turn your dreams into reality. The methods outlined in this book are not rocket science, but easy-to-follow steps that tell you how to format and complete a nonfiction book.

Whether you write about cooking, crafting, child care, retirement, or any other subject under the sun, and no matter how long the book is, the steps are similar. I know. I've written travel books; health books; books on death, destruction, and diseases; craft books; business books; fitness books; and cookbooks. Trust me — the same principles apply to all.

How the Publishing Process Works

Between the time an author gets a great idea to that moment when the book appears in your local bookstore, a great deal has occurred. So that you can begin to think and work like a publishing pro, here's an overview.

It's happened. You have a smashing, unique, intriguing, and marketable book idea. You have the feeling that it's the concept of a lifetime, and you're itching to get started. For this scenario only, let's say you want to write a cookbook filled with lore, legend, and recipes from the *Mayflower*. You remember that boat — it brought the Pilgrims to Plymouth Rock. You have an old recipe collection that's been passed down over the years and have heard all the stories of life back in the tough old days. Stick with me — it would be original. Because you're a savvy writer, you always take the following steps to achieve book-publishing victory.

Step 1. **You ponder the idea and the concept.** Sometimes this takes a few minutes; for some of us it takes years. Notice nothing has been written yet. At the right time, the idea will become fully developed in your mind. I promise you that will happen. I call this the speculation stage. Some writers refer to it as the gestation period before the book is born.

Step 2. **Research what has been written on your topic and what is already out in the market.** You can do this by scanning the pages of *Books in Print*, found at the library, and consulting online sources, such as the Internet bookstores Amazon.com and

BarnesandNoble.com. If you were researching this special cookbook, you would want to look up cookbooks that focus on New England historical recipes, cooking methods during Colonial times (we're talking open fires and smoky rooms), and the actual history of the Pilgrims as they suffered the hardships of settling their spot in the New World.

 ## Books in Print

Books in Print lists all books that are currently in print; that is, books that are currently available. It is organized by subject and title, as well as by author. Most libraries have copies.

Step 3. Read everything on your topic you can find easily. *Easily* is the operative word here because you'll have plenty of time once you get a publishing contract to delve into details. Your goal with Step 3 is to acquire a sound understanding of the topic so that you can write the book proposal. Don't do so much research at this step that you forget you are writing a book; you're not developing a footnoted research paper.

At this time, you'll want to list unusual terms or buzz words and understand them. In the case of a historical cookbook, you would probably want to update the recipes somewhat, because most chefs use products from the local supermarket and aren't able to go out and catch a muskrat or deer for dinner.

Step 4. You write a fantastic book proposal. Check out Chapter 9 to see how to do just that. A good book proposal takes from a week to three months, depending on how quickly you work.

Step 5. You send a perfect copy of the proposal to your agent. For recommendations on finding an agent, see

Chapter 10. Your agent is gaga over your idea and
assures you that a sale of the manuscript and a huge
advance are moments away.

Let's jump back to reality for a moment. Typically, agents
are hard-working, dedicated folks who are bogged down with
submittals, even from cherished clients, including you. Most
agents need a few weeks to get back to clients, and then they
might suggest some changes on the proposal. An agent will
not write the proposal for you. Agents market books and
writers write books. You get the idea.

Now, back to our scenario of an ideal world. The agent
immediately makes copies of the manuscript and delivers it
into the hands of favorite editors at nationally known
publishing houses. Within days, your agent calls with an offer
from one of the big publishing houses, like Random House, or
one of the smaller houses on the cutting edge, like Rodgers &
Nelsen. It's a great offer and you accept it.

Step 6. Wait.

While you wait, you begin to do more research and perhaps
some writing, but because you don't have a signed contract
yet, you try to be patient. This is smart business; unexpected
things often happen. During this step you organize your
materials and finish other work in progress so that you will
have time to work on the *Mayflower* cookbook when you have
a contract.

Step 7. The contract arrives and looks good. Your agent
discusses all the details. You sign it and send it to
your agent, who forwards it to the editor at the publishing house. Only then is the advance check issued.

**Step 8. With the advance check nestled snugly in your
bank account, you begin organizing and writing.**
Your contract said that you have twelve months to
finish the book. The length of time you have to write
a book is negotiable. Some contracts allow only six

weeks writing time; others can stretch out to eighteen months. You finish the book well before the deadline and send it either to your agent (some work this way) or directly to the editor, with whom you've bonded by now.

 ## Save Hours and Possibly Years

Make the most of telephone time. Chatting with friends on the phone is entertaining but a deadly time waster. Ditto for time-consuming e-mail, web browsing, and chat groups. Jot down notes on what you plan to cover when calling an editor, expert, or other writer. Try to keep all calls under three minutes.

Watch your spam consumption. *Spam* is junk e-mail that ranges from long-winded jokes to motivational babble. If you're not crazy about spam or if your computer system gets overloaded when you download the mail, tell friends and family, as politely as possible, to knock it off.

Step 9. Your editor gives your manuscript a first read and asks for some revisions. Don't take it personally — editors do this. It's your job to make those changes that enhance the book and discuss, that is, negotiate, the changes you believe detract from it.You do the work and return the manuscript on schedule.

Step 10. You receive a copy of the manuscript with even more questions and suggestions. This time the manuscript comes from the copy editor. You're usually working from a hard copy, so the pages with questions and problems are flagged with sticky notes. If you are working with electronic files, your publisher will flag the manuscript with a specific code so that you can search through and find the questions. For instance, in electronic editing, the equal sign (=)

marking a phrase typed in upper case letters might
indicate a query, such as, =DO YOU REALLY MEAN
CHILDREN ARE FREE? OR DO YOU MEAN
THAT CHILDREN MAY ATTEND THE EVENT
WITHOUT PAYING AN ADMISSION FEE?=

Finding mistakes and problems with your book is the copy
editor's job. The copy editor has to make sure that the
concepts, grammar, and format are clear. If the publisher uses
a specific style, your book must conform to that style, and
that's something the copy editor checks for too.

A few years ago I wrote *Resumes for Women* (Arco
Publishing). In the introduction I wrote about a five-point plan
to get a job. However, by the time I completed the book, I had
only four points to that plan, but even after careful proofread-
ing, I didn't see the *oops*. The editor didn't see the
discrepancy either; it was the ever-faithful copy editor who
pointed out the faux pas and saved our cookies.

**Step 11. You make the changes or clarify the concepts and
send it to the copy editor.**

Step 12. Wait.

**Step 13. You receive the galleys, which are the actual
printed sheets of your book's pages, typically
produced on oversized paper.** You know this is your
last chance to make any changes, and you also know
you'd better have a pretty good reason for making
them at this late date. Some publishers charge authors
for major changes made after the galleys are issued.

Even though the publisher has made you wait and wait,
when you receive the galleys, you have just days to read them.
When the galleys arrive you put all other work aside as you
peruse your golden words.

Your role is to find errors in the manuscript. You're another
pair of eyes, but you also know that you're not alone. A crew
of publishing professionals, from your editor to a proofreader,

is searching for typos too. You mark the errors in the specified way. You return the galleys and . . .

Step 14. Wait.

By now every member of your family is asking when the cookbook will be out, when you'll be doing signings, when you'll appear on *Oprah*. Of course, you have a tentative release date, but like babies and mortgage loan approvals, these dates are unpredictable. Instead of twiddling your thumbs, you make use of that spurt of excitement each time you hear a UPS truck drive down your street. You work on other projects, polish your public speaking skills, and write articles that you'll use to promote your book. You know the books will be coming any day, and time well managed is time well spent.

 ## Waiting for the Big Event

Once the book has been printed, it takes between four and eight weeks for copies to physically move out of a publisher's or printer's warehouse to bookstores. Sometimes it can take longer. For some archaic reason, it's not possible to rush this process. Sure, we've all seen books that are the result of some scandal make it to the stores in days, but for the rest of us, our precious babies take forever to be delivered.

Be mindful of the time it takes. Organize your promotional events and signings. You don't want to go on a book tour and not have the books at the stores when you arrive. You definitely don't want to write articles to promote your book and not have the book available for the consumer.

Step 15. Finally the UPS truck driver pulls to a stop at your house and delivers your free author's copies. Your book is a reality. What a moment. You don't know whether to cry or scream, so you do both. You wipe away tears of joy, jump up and down a few more times, and clutch the book to your chest. Then you exhale so deeply your knees feel weak. However, with a twist on that ever popular cliché: There's no rest for the wicked or for authors whose books have just arrived in stores. Because . . .

Step 16. The work now begins. You're ready because, while you waited throughout Steps 6, 12, and 14, you started to do preliminary publicity. (See Chapter 12 on ways you can help your publisher promote your book and make it a bestseller.)

The Reasons for and Rewards of Book Writing

If it takes months and, in many cases, years to write a book, why do it? There's no pat answer, and whatever feels right for you is the correct response.

I choose to write on topics that contribute to the betterment of humanity. Wow, that sounds highfalutin, yet it translates to mean I write about topics that help, inform, or entertain people. I write contemporary nonfiction how-to and self-help books with topics as varied as how to make crafts from scrap wood in *50 Wooden Crafts to Make with Kids* (Crown/Random House) to *What to Do When a Loved One Dies* (Dickens Press).

I write for money. After all, this is my profession, my day job, my real job. So don't think less of yourself if you, too, want to write for a living, as a career. You are not compromising your principles if you write for the money your words produce.

Other great reasons to write include a burning desire to say something to the world; to increase credibility, notoriety, or public awareness; and to entertain. Some people have the knack to blend all these motives and do it well. The late Erma Bombeck wrote humorously on subjects ranging from disciplining kids to keeping romance alive in a longtime relationship, and she made us laugh. Dave Barry and Andy Rooney do too.

If you're an expert in your field, you can gain credibility with the public by writing a book. Even in these times when everything seems electronic, print is not dead, and the public believes that anyone who has written a book is an authority. Want to see the truth of that statement? Watch some of the talk shows or listen to talk radio and you will be struck with how many "experts" have achieved overnight credibility, or in some cases, notoriety, upon the publication of their books.

Maybe the idea of writing a book just feels right in your soul. You need to write because you love words, your feelings spill onto the paper, and you want to create. If you've always known in your heart that you wanted to write a book, whether it's your memoirs or about a fascinating topic, then that's all the rationale you need. I believe this is the underlying reason most of us get into writing. We want to write something lengthy, meaty, and feel the need to complete a quest. As you talk with people about writing, perhaps when you're attending classes or conferences, you'll hear other reasons for writing, but that drive will probably be basic to all of them.

Now that you know why most people write books, let's look at the rewards. You could be on *Oprah*, you could help the public become aware of a sticky issue, you could share your philosophy, you could dispense information. The rewards, for most writers, center on personal satisfaction.

I've heard writing compared to giving birth to a child, yet I believe the process is more complex than that analogy implies. Creating a book is like rearing a child to become a successful, happy adult. In the parenting process and the writing process there are no universal answers: Each child and book is distinctive. You can get opinions on how to do it. You can talk with experts and get books on the topics, much like the one you have in your hands. But both parenting and writing require that you put in time, attention, love, and care, and, eventually, you must set that child or book free.

As a parent, your reward is seeing your child do well, independently, in the big, wide world. As writers, we feel the same rush of gratification when we see our books at the bookstore or library. If that book is mentioned or reviewed by a magazine or newspaper, our hearts soar. When bestseller status is possible or a literary prize is likely, and everyone is chatting about that book, there is no reward on the planet to match the pride the writer feels.

The reward for writing a book feels similar to overcoming a hurdle because it produces greater self-confidence. It feels great to be a writer and see your book in print.

Planning Your Nonfiction Book's Success

Let's add a twist to this old saw: Good things come to those who . . . have tenacity. When you begin pondering the type of book you want to write and sell, you need to plan for its future. When this book was still in the writing stage, and after an especially trying day, Craig Nelsen, the publisher of this series, asked me, "Will the series be a success?" I laughed, and he laughed when I replied, "Boy, I wouldn't be working this hard if I thought I could fail."

Writing is work. It's hard work. Only dreamers think they can write a book, call a publisher, and in a wink have the book on the *New York Times* bestseller list. We've all met these wishful thinkers; the next time you talk with one, be gentle, and then continue to do your work.

As a writer, it is essential to be aware of trends in publishing and the public's views. That means you'll want to keep up to date on current events, fads, and philosophies that are affecting our lives. If you forget this, you could attempt to write and sell a book few people will want to buy. Thinking of writing a book on how to dance the disco? Yes, it may come back again, but it's definitely not as hot as it was in the 1970s when John Travolta first stuck his arm in the air.

Some topics are tied to the times, such as disco, yet others are constantly in demand. Books on business, parenting, relationships, how-tos, travel, and inspirational topics transcend fads. We'll talk more about how to choose a marketable topic for your blockbuster in the next chapter. For now, let's concentrate on your favorite subject: you.

1. To make your book a success, you must have tenacity.

When I wrote my first book, *60-Second Shiatzu* (Mills & Sanderson and Henry Holt Publishers), I'd been writing for magazines for a number of years, but I pined (read *lusted*) for a book I could call my own. My first book topic had to do with Japanese acupressure. It came about after I took a class on the technique and then wrote some articles about it. I figured out what was then a new angle on the subject. With research and study, I made it a book with a quick twist.

Because this was my first book, I had no idea what I was doing or about writing a proposal. I wrote the entire manuscript. I showed it to, sent it out to, tried to contact, 49 — count 'em, 49 — publishers. No sale. Some publishers weren't even civil.

It probably doesn't surprise you to discover that I didn't stop. I continued with a steadfastness demonstrated by Hannibal, who crossed the Alps with elephants, and Harriet Beecher Stowe, who brought the scourge of slavery to the public's notice. I would not be thrown off my course for success. Failure was simply not an option.

It took about a year, and finally the fiftieth publisher, Mills & Sanderson in Bedford, Massachusetts, loved the book and bought it. They didn't know at that time how far down my contact list they were, but they were obviously the right choice.

Since that time in the mid-1980s, *60-Second Shiatzu* has gone into six printings for Mills & Sanderson and has been

published in fifteen foreign countries, distributed throughout
the United Kingdom by Simon and Schuster, and chosen as a
Quality Paperback Book Club selection. About two years ago
the book sold to Henry Holt Publishers for a new life and two
reprinted editions.

If I had stopped at 20 rejections or 30 or even 49, I would
never have had this success nor the other good things that
initial success has brought, like selling books on more than 40
different topics. The basic truth here is, you cannot be a
quitter and a writer too. The two are not compatible. If at any
time during the writing, selling, and promoting process, you
feel like quitting, pretend I'm right there with you. If I were,
I'd tell you straight out, "Remember *60-Second Shiatzu*. Dust
off your boots, my dear, and get back in the game. It's the
only way to win."

Now a Word from Your Coach

"It's not whether you get knocked down. It's
whether you get up again," said football coach
Vince Lombardi.

If you write books for a living, you will get knocked
down. Sometimes getting rejected is painful — our egos
get bruised — but the alternative is to lie there, never
really knowing if you could have made it.

2. To make your book a success, you must be able to write.

Contrary to what someone may have once told you, writing
a book doesn't require a fancy degree from an ivy-covered
college. It requires the ability to put sentences down in a
logical order and to engage the reader. Period.

The skill of writing well can be learned. Some folks have a
gift that makes it child's play; the rest of us require practice. I
look back to the books I wrote early in my career and realize
that twenty years later, I'm a much better writer. Twenty years
of practicing anything from soccer to the piano will make you

much better at it, and writing is included in that list.

When I teach the university course, "How to Write the Nonfiction Book," I push my students to write every single day on their nonfiction books in progress, on essays, or even on ramblings in personal journals. "But what if it's not good enough?" is usually the retort heard during the first hour of the first class. Well, that's what the *Delete* key and erasers are for.

Remember, physicians practice medicine, lawyers practice law, musicians practice music. We book writers practice our skills too.

 Get Out of Here

Want to think more clearly and come up with some fresh ideas? Every writer needs to take regular breaks. Go for a short walk, right now, if only for five minutes. Get out of the office during your writing day.

When you're walking, straighten your posture, breathe deeply, and swing your arms. Go once around the garden, up and down a flight of stairs, or to the end of the block and back. Repeat this any time you need to clear your mind.

If you're absolutely, positively not the type to walk, stretching is also great to get the brain cells functioning again.

3. To make your book a success, you must constantly improve yourself.

Only you know the personal areas that need to be enhanced to make you a better writer and eventually a promoter of your bestseller. I was a shy teenager and an awkward young adult. I've had to struggle with shyness ever since my writing propelled me into the spotlight of radio, television, and speaking engagements. I've worked hard to become comfortable enough to speak in front of crowd.

Whether you're timid, computer-phobic, need to brush up on grammar, or have any other real or perceived obstacle to your success, take time to improve yourself. Seek and get the advice you need now, early in your writing career, and you'll never wonder if that obstacle held you back from achieving your goal.

Pick a Color

Choose any color. Now, in the first person, write about your choice. Write at least 50 words before you stop. Do not edit as you write; just let it flow.

Here's a sample. Yes, you can use blue if you really have to, but choosing a wild color like puce, chartreuse, or maize forces you to stretch those creative muscles.

I am a Montana sky. Infinite. I am the Maui coastline filled with the creatures of the universe. I am the Atlantic Ocean, angry and lurching at Nova Scotia, irresistible and frigid and ever changing.

I am an old-fashioned jar of Vick's Vapo-Rub sitting on a shelf, waiting for the anxious parent of a sniffing child. I am bachelor's buttons, cornflowers, the background on a computer screen. I am blue.

CHAPTER 2

Increasing Your Odds for Success

*The best way to get a good idea
is to get a lot of ideas.*
— Linus Pauling

"If only it were easy to write and sell a nonfiction book." I overheard this wishful comment at a recent writers' conference. And I silently added, "Well, if it were easy, everybody's uncle, mother, sister, and coworker would be working on one and selling it too."

It's hard work to write, and there's more to writing than just writing. We have to figure out what's going to be hot in the future, because the future is when our books will hit the shelves. It's essential that we understand how to determine the marketability of our topics. We need to make sure our ideas are fresh, bright, and original, and we have to have a strong business sense.

In this chapter you'll learn the how-tos and what-fors to help you focus on writing, marketing, and making it as a writer in the future. We will cover the hot topics of nonfiction books and how to determine the market success of your topic before you write a single word. Only an imaginary crystal ball is needed, along with great common sense and the intuition you already have. You will also discover how to check your innovative ideas against reality and factor in your success to this winning equation.

Today's and Tomorrow's Hottest Book Topics

Americans are fickle book buyers and readers. It's no news that we're swayed by what's happening in the media, with movie stars, and with pop culture fads. Such rapidly shifting trends make predicting the next bestseller a challenge.

Walk your eyes down the *New York Times* bestseller list, and you'll have a pretty good idea of what Americans are buying now. Go a step further, with a real walk around a major bookstore, and that idea will become clearer. Initially you might think you could write a book on any old topic, even Mesopotamian casserole cooking, and get it published. Not so by a long shot. Your book has to be placed in a recognizable niche, or the book will not do well.

Publishers attempt to foretell what we'll be reading a year or so into the future, and these are the only types of books they're interested in. Savvy writers know they must play this foretelling game too, so that they can propose book ideas that publishers want.

Depending on where you are in your career, you might have a publisher call and ask you to put together a proposal or develop a book concept on a specific topic. That's what all book writers dream of happening. For most of us, we have to do it the old-fashioned way: Watch the trends and use our best intuitive skills to predict what will sell six to eighteen months in the future when our books are released.

Predicting reading trends is not really that difficult. Here's the secret: Americans like specific types of books, although their tastes in topics shift. For instance, in the early 1990s, diet books were hot. Everyone from the buxom lifeguards on popular TV shows to Dr. Whosit with a clinic in Waukegan came out with an unhealthy and faddish diet. Some of these books sold like hot cakes.

Times have changed, and we've become better informed about safe, and risky, ways to treat our bodies. Today, however, weight loss books are still selling well, and a good third of all Americans still weigh more than is healthy.

Nowadays most people want a diet designed by someone with a medical or nutritional degree, and they want a sound weight reduction program. You get the point: While the concept remains strong, the focus has changed.

The same goes for everything from craft books to sports books. We want the basic information and the story behind the story. This a trend in writing that you'll see instantly when you begin researching contemporary books on your topic.

Some trends are being shaped by that huge segment of our reading population, the baby boomers. With the arrival of the first gray hair, many of us are taking a serious look at the future, from retirement planning to mutual funds to anti-aging formulas. If you're a baby boomer, identify what you're concerned about and you'll find that a lot of people are inclined to agree. Issues surrounding the aging of the baby boomers will probably continue to be hot for the next ten to fifteen years.

The topics that are most popular right now, and are likely to continue into the future, are those on everyone's mind. We want to do everything easier, have more spare time, be smarter, have extra income, and be more attractive. Fill that bill and you've got a good idea. Today's hottest topics include the following.

1. Information — From Computer Tips to Household Tips. As newspapers and the evening news shout ever more loudly about how dangerous life is "out there," more people are spending time at home. Hot topics include anything related to the house, from converting that old shed into a ballroom to adding a gym in the attic. Find ways to make a chore or career easier, quicker, and more fun and you'll have a good topic.

2. Self-Improvement. Help people find lasting love, get a great wardrobe at the thrift store, or become a better person, and the book will practically sell itself.

3. Food. Forget a collection of recipes or a modification of concepts that have been around the kitchen stove more than once. Again, make the preparation quicker and more fun and throw in some history or romance of the food or its preparation, and you'll have a viable book. Ethnic cooking constantly gains in popularity, as do collections of homey recipes. A few years ago the trend in cookbooks was to tell us how to reduce the fat in foods. Cooking "lite" was hot and we all got the message. Now it's unusual to see any modern cookbooks encouraging us to pour fat-laden gravies over slabs of meat. Looking into our book-writing crystal ball, I predict more food books that are a blend of travel, a memoir, and recipes, much like Laura Esquivel's bestseller, *Like Water for Chocolate* (Doubleday). The cookbook of the future will tell a story and stand by itself as a good read.

4. Travel and Adventure. Nonfiction books about adventures will continue to be popular for the next ten years — and it doesn't take our crystal ball to see that. A recent survey estimated that air travel will increase by 50 percent by 2007. You'll be moving in the right direction if you write about an adventure that's truly different, like climbing peaks in Nepal, forging along in the Amazon, or walking across America. Or you might want to consider blending a personal saga with recipes, humor, or how-tos. Travel and adventure books can also include stories of families traveling together. If their reasons for being on the road are altruistic, for example, if they are helping to build homes for the needy, your proposal may appeal to a publisher on several levels and have a good chance of being accepted.

Conversely, if you're planning to write about your trip to San Francisco where you stayed in a fancy hotel and took in the sights of the city by the bay, good luck. Although your visit may have been fun, you'll have a tough time convincing a publisher that such a commonplace experience is worth the expense to publish the book. (Please see Publishing Is Expensive box later in this chapter.)

5. Celebrity Books. We love to know about the folks we see on the big and small screens and those people who make news.

Tell-all books will continue to be popular until the day publishing ceases to exist. If you have a connection with a celebrity, or are an expert in a related field (for example, if your other job is costume design for films) and can sprinkle stardust on your topic, you might have something. Remember, celebrity books are not just about movie people; you can write about anyone who, for *any* reason, is in the limelight.

6. Parenting Books. A large part of the reading public is either experiencing the joys and frustration of being first-time parents or having aging parents to care for. Books about families, and specifically parenting, will continue to be marketable for the next decade. Readers want to know how others cope, and they want to hear the secrets of others' success. Don't forget that family shapes are continuously changing and blending — adoptive and non-traditional families are dealing with parenting issues.

7. Pets. Many of us live with animal companions who fill the roles of family and friends. If you can write about pets and know your topic, you'll have a good chance with a book, whether it's on canine CPR and first aid or how to breed prize-winning parrots. You could also go more deeply into the human-animal bond, and even explore the psychological or psychic aspects of animals.

8. Work and Career. If you've left your corporate job and opened a successful one-person business and you can share your how-tos and some of the pitfalls, conveying it all in a motivational writing style, then you have a fine topic for a book of the future. Again, if you can tell the reader how to do something more easily, with more pleasure to it, and find more spare time, then you'll be set for publishing a book.

9. Money. Right next to love, money is on everyone's mind. If you can write about how to make more or use it wisely, and do it in an innovative manner, then you'll find success.

10.Inspirational and New Age Topics. Last in the line of hot

topics, the inspirational market is stronger than it has ever been
in my recollection. It's essential to know your field well when
writing for the inspirational and religious markets. Each has
specialty languages. In these genres, simpler is often better,
and simple is often successful. Cases in point are *Simple
Abundance* (Warner) and *Don't Sweat the Small Stuff*
(Hyperion). For more information about writing for these
markets, see Chapter 5. Also included in this category are hot
subtopics of alternative medicine and complementary
therapies, and paranormal fields; publishing houses
specializing in these genres will continue to produce
opportunities for writers.

Now that you've read about the topics that are popular today
and will continue to be so, unless the poles shift or Martians
land, think of how you'll put your own twist on them.
Remember, you are your book and the way you write it is what
will or will not make it sell.

Was it Dorothy Parker, Yogi Berra, or the Biblical preacher
of Ecclesiastes who said, "There's nothing new under the
sun"? Smart writers heed this adage. They revisit the wisdom
of the ages, give it a face-lift, and add a contemporary twist
here and there. Then they rake in the profits of a hot book
topic.

 ## Do You Need an Attitude Adjustment?

Put a few writers together and sooner or later the
conversation turns to that old bugaboo usually
referred to as *dealing with rejection.* Yes, I've
been disappointed when an editor says, "No thanks" to one
of my proposals. I learned very early in my writing life not
to dwell on such things or take them personally.

When my idea is rejected, it means that my proposal
simply didn't fit that editor's needs. It doesn't make me a
bad writer or stupid or a failure. I have more ideas, which I
can either propose to that editor or to another one.

I'm reminded of what happened when I decided to put a new fence in the back of my home situated on a suburban quarter acre. Visions of fences that were attractive, sturdy, rustic, and yet affordable danced in my mind as I got proposals from three contractors. I chose the one who seemed to have the right combination of experience, the best materials, and the time to do the job when I needed it completed.

It's unlikely that the two people who didn't get the job spent more than two minutes pondering why they didn't win the contract. Can you imagine a contractor going into a royal blue funk because she didn't get to build my fence? Isn't it funny to imagine a carpenter looking glum and wondering if he was a failure because I didn't call back with a yes? Without a doubt the contractors who didn't get the job were far too busy organizing the jobs they did have and creating new proposals.

Follow my lead on this one. You're in business just like those fencing contractors, and you need to move ahead instead of wondering if you're a flop and how and why your proposal didn't score a contract.

Determining a Book's Marketability

Writing a book goes well beyond putting provocative sentences together, regardless of how many sentences it takes. To sell a book, you must have a marketable topic.

When teaching the course, "How to Write the Nonfiction Book," I have my students go on a field trip to a large bookstore. Their assignment is to walk around and discover where their future bestsellers will be placed on the shelves.

I always get some flak before a bookstore trip with comments such as, "But my book is so unique, I can't put it with the others." Or, "There's no competition for my topic. It's never been done before." Fine and dandy — your book might be special. But if the sales clerk at the bookstore can't figure out in which section to place your book, it may be shelved incorrectly and will sell fewer copies.

Of course, this doesn't mean you have to write to a formula. That's the beauty of our creative minds — we can all figure out a twist for even the most mundane topic. Still, you must find an established niche for your book. Let's say you're planning a collection of wit and wisdom on parenting, as I did with the Health Communications book, *For the Love of Children.* At the bookstore, you discover your book could be sold in the parenting section, but it could also be sold with books filled with quotations.

 ## Careful Critiques

There's danger in letting a loved one read your writing.

Even if you have an ego like Napoleon's, it could be perilous to have a loved one critique your work. Don't do it, even if the person has a degree in English.

If you let your loved one read your pre-published work, one of several things can happen. (1) You'll get a biased opinion. "Darling, I love you and love all of your writing." All that kiss-kiss, gush-gush, love-you stuff is not any real help at all. Or (2) you will get an opinion that is too critical, because of such underlying issues as a touch of resentment toward your possible success in a field as weird as writing. "You don't mind if I rip this to shreds, do you, Darling? There are just, oh, five hundred words I'd like to correct." Or (3) even if your beloved knows the English language, maybe the genre you're working in is a total mystery to that person.

Instead, critique your own work, or network with writers in your genre for a helpful manuscript evaluation. One of the best ways to improve your writing is to join a critique group of other writers. Check with your local library, university, or community college to see if such a group already exists. If it doesn't, start one yourself.

As you begin to think about marketability, consider whether there have been successful books similar to yours. For example, if you're planning to write on backyard vegetable gardening, and the current bestseller lists top off with a book on this same topic, that's great news. It means that consumers want to read about this subject. Your job is to make your book even more appealing than the competition. We'll talk more about this when we identify your reader in Chapter 6 and discuss the book proposal in Chapter 9. Don't get jittery. You'll discover that the process of making your book happen is not only possible, but simple and easy to understand, too.

Checking Out the Competition

Some nonfiction book writers are so original in their thinking that they can just take hold of their topics, let the creativity flow, and out stream the words. They never figure out how to analyze their markets, find a twist, or position their books for success. The darnedest thing is that sometimes this approach works. If you've been using this method and your book is finished and it is being published and you're happy with the result, skip this section.

Most of the rest of us mortals need a plan and need to see what else is out there before we can figure our twist, or at least confirm, that we do have something new to say. You do this by checking out the competition.

Your library is a beginner's source. And lots of beginning writers limit their research of the competition to a perusal of the shelves of the local library. That's naive and dangerous to the success of a book project because libraries often lack the kind of wide selection of current nonfiction titles you will find in a big bookstore. It's a sad fact of life that most libraries are underfunded and "under-booked" and often don't have the latest editions because taxpayers "under-approve" bond issues. To really find out about competitive books, you must visit a large bookstore. The Internet bookstores work well too, but a field trip to a large bookstore, as mentioned earlier, is your best source of information.

You'll also want to put on your reading glasses and trudge through *Books in Print*; in Chapter 1 you learned about this reference that lists currently available books. *Books in Print* is organized by subject, title, and author, and most public libraries and some bookstores have them.

Try to get a handle on your close competition. You'll need to know about these books when you're writing the book proposal.

Books in Print — A Navigational Nightmare?

Sometimes wading through *Books in Print* can be a daunting process. When you're looking through thousands of books, how do you separate the wheat from the chaff?

A good clue is the publishing date. If you find a book currently in print that seems to be in direct competition with your idea, look a little further. There's a good chance the publishing date might be several years old, sometimes as much as fifty years old. The book may still be in print, but it's unlikely that the information in it will have a contemporary focus.

Once you've seen the books that are in competition with your book, your job is to gather enough information and format your idea in a way that is totally fresh. You should have a good idea of how your idea is unique — perhaps you present innovative concepts, new research, or a scientific discovery. A publisher will not buy your book on your statement, "My book has an unconventional slant." In your words, your outline, and the marketing section of your proposal, you have to prove that what you can provide is unusual.

How can you discover a fresh slant? It's accomplished through research and study. As stuffy as this might seem, concentrated exploration of your subject is the only way. You must keep up with trends, which can be found everywhere from the *Journal of Nursing* to *People* magazine. You can also interview experts who are on the cutting edge of the field. You can do your own studies and polls. You can simplify a complex topic. All these techniques can help make your idea unique.

When *The Successful Writer's Guide to Publishing Magazine Articles* (Rodgers & Nelsen) first came out, I gave a lecture to beginning writers. The day after the lecture, a determined novice e-mailed me the message, "Thanks for your book. Unlike the other books on writing for magazines I've read, it's written without pretension. It's in plain English." It was his remark of "plain English" that pleased me most. I'd achieved my goal.

There have been other books on how to write for magazines, but mine gives information in a way everyone can use. That was the twist I took on that topic and, judging from the response, it worked.

Factoring Your Success

As you begin to research your book's success-ability, it's time to think about your own. I know it's not fair, but we are judged by how we look and how we speak. Today, the book publisher's Authors from Heaven are articulate people who can hold audiences in the palms of their hands, have great rapport with the media, and understand that, to sell books, writers have to move away from their comfort zones. I would estimate that half of the beginning writers who have been in my classes are not comfortable giving speeches or talking to the media, yet somehow they believe their nervousness will disappear once they become famous authors.

In the business of writing nonfiction books, you have to be a marketing master and seek out ways to exploit the sales of your book. Sure, the publisher will do some promotion, but they also expect you to spend time and money on promoting

your own product. For some people that means signing a
check for a public relations specialist to create press kits,
design seminars, and arrange tours and radio and television
interviews. For the rest of us, it means that while in the
process of writing the book, we're already looking at
promotional opportunities and ways to improve our public
images. We may never feel completely comfortable in front of
a camera or 500 people, but we can learn to do it.

 Dress for Success

As you're getting ready for your next
appointment to interview an expert, to drop a
manuscript off at an agent or publisher's office,
or to go to a writers' conference, take another look in your
mirror. Would you hire the person you see in the reflection,
strictly on appearances alone? Judging a book or person by
the cover is unfair — every grown-up knows that. But we
also know that life isn't always fair.

Therefore, regardless of what you wear in your home
office, make sure you have two or three professional outfits,
simple or sophisticated, clean and neat, when you go out for
business reasons.

Dress according to the situation. If I were meeting an
editor on Park Avenue in New York City, I would wear my
most business-like attire. If that editor and I were meeting at
a cafe here in San Diego during her vacation, I'd dress more
casually because a suit and silk blouse wouldn't be right for
the location.

If your appearance is appropriate and professional, only
your work will be evaluated, and people won't remember
you as that writer who came in with dirty sneakers, worn-out
jeans, and a sweater that had seen better days.

When you look like a professional, you act more
professional.

You may want to hire a fashion consultant, learn new make-up skills, have your hair style updated, get contact lenses, or take voice lessons. You might want to join Toastmasters or take a public speaking class at your local community college.

Before every public appearance I get a case of butterflies. Instead of running away, I use that feeling to energize myself. I practice smiling, when I'm alone; practice my presentation, again, when I'm alone; and then figure out what I'll wear. Few successful authors wear shabby sweaters and scuffed up shoes, although that might be the image some people still have of the creative writer. Most of the time I wear a blue or red suit when speaking and something slightly more casual when signing books at trade shows and in bookstores. My goal for the costume of a "famous writer" — what I jokingly call *dress-up clothes* — is to be approachable. I want you to come up and talk with me, shake my hand, and, of course, buy a book. That's why all authors do public appearances.

If you're not yet comfortable with a public role, use the time while you write your book to focus on yourself. It will pay big dividends.

Advances and Royalties

Isn't it amazing that people will share the intimate details of their romantic lives but won't divulge how much money they make? Go figure. The same is true of most writers. And this hush-hush philosophy stops us from knowing if we're making competitive wages. But now the cat is about to be let out of the bag.

You may have heard the words *advance* and *royalty* bantered around. Everyone has read about the huge amounts of money that Stephen King and Amy Tan get for their novels. And when any famous or notorious political leader spills his guts in a memoir, the figures are astounding.

Advances range from nonexistent to hefty amounts in the millions of dollars. The average writer with the average book can expect to receive a $5,000 to $50,000 advance depending on the topic, publisher, and credentials of the author. The amount of the advance also depends on how hot the trend is for the book.

Let's go over a bit of background first. An advance from a publisher is an advance in money against future royalties. Your book will have to generate enough sales, according to the percentages spelled out in your contract, to repay the advance before you begin to earn royalties.

Pen Names — Who Needs 'Em?

Why would a writer use a pen name? Often it's done to conceal a writer's identity for one reason or another; sometimes it's done to make the book or topic more appealing. When a colleague, Sissy, began writing a book on the fundamentals of language, she used her given name rather than the nickname everyone called her and which she uses for writing magazine articles. Her full, legal name gives her work more credibility.

If you choose to use a pen name, for whatever purpose, be sure to let the editor know. If you will always be writing under an alias, you may have to file a fictitious name statement with your city and advertise it in the newspaper before your bank will honor checks made out to your pen name.

Review the legal ramifications. Remember, too, the publisher plans to have you do publicity. While you may be able to write using a pen name, will you be a hit on the talk shows wearing a hat and veil or a brown paper bag over your head to hide your real identity?

If you're working with an agent, the advance and royalty checks go to your agent first, who takes out 10 to 15 percent, depending on your agreement. Then your agent issues you an agency check. Don't worry. If your brilliant book doesn't sell enough copies to pay back the advance, you are not liable to

return any money. That's part of the risk a publisher takes
when doing business.

You can't judge a book deal by the amount of the advance
because you have to look at the other elements of your
contract. The smaller the advance, the sooner it will be repaid
and the sooner you'll receive royalty checks on a regular basis.
You might think that a large advance would motivate the
publisher to pay attention to promoting your book, so the
advance would be repaid quickly with book sales, but don't
count on that as a barometer. A smaller advance with a high-
quality, highly organized, and well-known publisher or an up-
and-coming publisher might be the right decision for you. A
small advance with a brand new publisher who really makes
you feel like a big fish in a small pond has advantages too,
especially for your first book. With a new, smaller publisher
you'll learn the ropes and feel comfortable asking questions.
You could get lost dealing with a larger publisher.

I've been published by some of the biggest publishing
houses, and I've been published by smaller ones. With each
book deal, I look at the money. Then I find out how the house
plans to sell my book, where and how advertising will be
directed, and how they treat authors.

Let's say for a minute that you're a public speaker with a
good client list. The downside is that you know you can only
speak at so many conferences in one year. Every time you
finish in front of the microphone, the crowd is fired up and
they clamor around you to buy your book. Oops. No book.
No extra income. You know you're losing contacts and actual
income. So you write a book and sign with a big publishing
house. You like the fact that you can tell the world that XYZ is
your publisher. The advance is good, in the $30,000 range.
Because of the book deal, you figure it will take about a year
to pay back the advance and see royalties. Okay, you can wait.

Now let's change the scenario. You're a popular public
speaker and travel around the country giving motivational
seminars. At the end of each seminar, you sell boatloads of
books about your rags-to-riches story. You had offers from the

big houses, but you went with a smaller publisher because you wanted to take control of much of the marketing. The deal you cooked up with the publisher is that you can buy copies of the book at a significant discount and resell them to your public. Your profit is about $10 a copy for each book sold at the seminars — that's around $6 more for each book than you would receive from royalties alone. And best of all, you get royalties for the books too. Furthermore, you opted for a small advance, so you are now at the highest level of royalty percentages.

 ## Publishing Is Expensive

It's expensive to publish a book and that's exactly why publishers are *ultra* careful about the books they buy and the people they hire to write them.

It costs about $12,000 to actually buy the paper and print 5,000 copies of a book. It costs about $2,000 to $5,000 for a graphic artist to design the cover and create the page look. An editor is paid from $30,000 to $80,000 a year, and will work on a book for about four months. In this case, let's imagine that the writer receives a $50,000 advance.

We're talking about $100,000 just for the book, even before it gets to the publisher's warehouse. Add to that the costs of shipping to distributors and bookstores, advertising and other media coverage, and an author tour. Look at advertising alone: A page in *USA Today* runs about $100,000. A small print ad in a lesser-known magazine goes for $250 and up.

When you do the math, as the editor must do while deciding on the future of your book proposal, it makes perfect sense for publishers to be careful selecting books, topics, and authors.

Either of these two examples might be the right scenario for you. You have to weigh all your book deal options, because the amount of the advance isn't everything.

So how much money can you expect to make as a writer of books? That depends on who you are. If you can only write one book every ten years, but receive a $100,000 advance, your yearly writing income is a skinny $10,000. The average full-time writer can make an annual income in the range of $40,000, provided writing is actually that person's full-time occupation. Keep in mind that all people in the arts, including writers, can't equate success with a dollar sign. If you love your writing job, have no commute, can set your own hours, and feel wonderful seeing your books in print, then you are a success regardless of your yearly income.

To be truthful, most book writers supplement their income by writing articles. For more information about writing articles, see *The Successful Writer's Guide to Publishing Magazine Articles* (Rodgers & Nelsen), the companion book to this one. Writers may also teach writing classes, coach writing students, and hold other day jobs. I do all those things, including being a ghostwriter for some notable clients. Yet every single day, as I'm counting my blessings, I'm gratified to know that I get paid to do what I love — write.

 *Be Serious*

English author and actor Peter Ustinov said, "Comedy is simply a funny way of being serious." In my favorite film, What About Bob, Bill Murray plays the character of a paranoid guy who turns out to be smarter than a pompous psychiatrist. The serious note here, for me, is that not everyone marches to the same drumbeat. As the Beaver's brother, Wally Cleaver, said, "It's okay to be goofy."

Think about your favorite funny movie or episode of a TV series. For the next five minutes, write about the serious message it shares. Write about how that message touched you in some way.

CHAPTER 3

Making Sure You Are Qualified to Write

You may write for the joy of it, but the act of writing is not complete in itself. It has its end in its audience.

— Flannery O'Connor

You've probably heard people, who are not writers, say that they could easily write a book. I'm sure they can manipulate a pen or a computer keyboard, but what most don't know is that the more training you have to write, the better writer you will be. That means you'll have a much easier time selling your book.

In this chapter I'll walk you through the need-to-know writing tips that will help you become more qualified at this trade. I'm going to share with you some tricks writing teachers often neglect to give. Often, professors assume, "My goodness, *everyone* knows that." Everybody does not know this stuff.

In this chapter you'll learn how to use punctuation and grammar to your best interest. You'll get a crash course on how fiction techniques can put a spark in your books. I'll describe the real way to format and present a manuscript to a publisher. We'll also explore different types of nonfiction writing styles. If you're already writing your nonfiction book, flip straight to the section entitled, Manuscript Format and Preparation, which appears later in this chapter, to make sure you're formatting your book correctly.

 ## Writing and Learning by Mail

Look through any writer's magazine, and you'll find plenty of choices for writing courses available through *distance learning,* the method we used to refer to as *correspondence courses.*

Distance learning is the right choice for busy adults who already have a life and have little time to return to school. For some prospective writers, even attending a writing class at night is out of the question.

Before you enroll in any distance learning writing course, be a wise consumer. Check the school's references, find out about the credentials of the instructors, ascertain the timetable of assignments, and discuss money issues. Such programs as the Long Ridge Writer's Group return all your tuition if you're not satisfied.

Yes, with a good instructor, you can become a better writer via the mail or the modem.

The Importance of Writing Clearly

We've established that you don't need a wall covered with diplomas or a credential from Harvard to be a writer. So what does it take to be one? It takes heaping measures of tenacity and the ability to construct a clear, purposeful sentence.

English is tricky. Why do we spell *read* and *reed* differently but pronounce the words identically? And how about *saw* (the verb *to see*) and *saw* (the cutting tool)? In what other language would you yell, "Duck!" to warn someone to take cover? Why not *cow* or *yellow*? Ah, the mysteries of our native tongue.

If English isn't your native language or you honestly believe that you need some work in this area, enroll in an English composition class at a community college near you. Or sign up for a distance learning course where you can connect online to an English class that will help you over real or imagined obstacles.

The best way to learn about writing marketable nonfiction is to read nonfiction that has already been published. If, for example, you're planning to write how-to books in the contemporary, friendly writing style that's popular today, study a few dozen of the most popular ones to note the punctuation, sentence structure, and style they have in common. Don't read how-to books that have been around for ten or even five years. Many of these older books wouldn't sell in today's highly competitive market because the language is stuffy.

 ## Save Bucks on Books

Who doesn't love a bargain? Save from 5 to 20 percent when you buy books from a publisher or self-published author by asking if there are any slightly damaged books available for sale.

As you may know, bookstores and book distributors like Ingram or Baker and Taylor will not sell slightly damaged books for the retail market. But you can sometimes get books directly from the publisher for a song. So if you're not fussy about a bit of bruising on a book you want or need, then try this money saving tip.

Tools of the Trade

Every profession has tools. Engineers and mathematicians use numbers. Graphic designers and interior designers use computers and colors, shapes, and forms. Gardeners use lawn mowers and hedge clippers. A writer's tools are words. Just as a carpenter would never be able to cut a two-by-four with a hammer, a writer who uses the wrong writing tool — an inappropriate style or the wrong word or punctuation mark — won't get the job done either.

To speak to your reader and clarify the images that are in your head, you need the tools of words. If you're rusty or haven't ever thought of words as your tools, then review the tips for writing clear sentences shown here.

- **Vary sentence types and lengths to make reading interesting.** Simple sentences always work. Here's an example of a simple sentence: "She was smart." Compound sentences are simply two simple sentences joined by a conjunction, such as *and, but, or,* and *yet.* Therefore, a compound sentence might read like this: "She was smart and she knew it." A complex sentence adds a phrase to a simple sentence. "Although she never gambled, she was smart." And then there are compound-complex sentences that pull in both facets of this technique, such as, "Although she never gambled, she was smart, and at the start of horse racing season, she developed a method to win."

- **Use varying sentence structures to build tension or to identify people who are talking within your text.** If you want to convey a feeling of anxiety you might write:

  At first, he couldn't place the sound. Footsteps. Yes, they were footsteps. They were faint, all right, but there. They sounded like a 40-piece drum band echoing in his brain, pounding through his ears, spooking him to the core, and if he'd had time to think, he would have recognized the slightly off-beat tempo. With a start, he knew it was Max. Max was bad news.

- **Eva's general rules of writing:**

  1. If a typed sentence runs more than three lines, cut it in two.
  2. If paragraphs go over eight to ten typewritten lines, they are too long. Break them up.
  3. Always keep your reader in mind when you're writing. Please see Chapter 6 for more information on how to do this, the easy way.

- **It's okay to break the sentence and paragraph writing rules once you know them.** Your writing job is to produce words in a way that the reader can comprehend the images you've created. However, if you have too many disjointed phrases or too many compound-complex sentences, your writing is going to be difficult to understand.

- **Use 5-cent words rather than 50-cent ones.** If you're writing contemporary nonfiction, always remember that Americans prefer to read at a sixth-grade level. Don't misunderstand this inclination. We're not dull-witted. But when we want information, we want it quickly and without pretension.

If your writing is cluttered with labyrinthine paragraphs and elongated utterances in the form of multifarious sentences, editors will only be impressed with how much your writing style is outdated. Most likely, your work will be sent directly back to you. So if you have tendencies in this direction, change to a simpler style.

 ## Editing for the Better

When golden words must go, don't do it too quickly.

We all have writing foibles. *One* of mine, which is not revealed in the final copy that goes to an editor, is a tendency for sweetness to creep into even the tightest corners of a well-written manuscript. Phrases rhyme and adjectives effervesce. I've had paragraphs become as sugary as double-Dutch chocolate cake with a whipped cream center and two inches of gooey mocha frosting on the top.

Word images are great — we strive for imagery — yet personally, I have to guard against overdoing it, or my reader will feel bilious.

Don't think you're deficient if you too suffer from composing sentences that are all too cute, pretentious, or

eloquent. If any words or sentences do not carry the
theme of your piece, are not in the same voice as the
entire manuscript, or are absolutely, positively
breathtakingly beautiful, select that phrase and hit *Move*.
Don't strike the *Delete* key. Start a file on your hard
drive or disk with "extras" that you've cut from your
book, but aren't quite ready to send to alphabet heaven.

This file becomes a holding bin for cast-off words and
ideas. I've found that some are worthy of being recycled,
at which point I look back at the bin and identify places to
re-insert them. The Publishing Is Expensive box in
Chapter 2 is a case in point. It was cut from one part of
this book, saved, and then stuck in the right place as I was
doing some editing.

Be ruthless with your editing, but be wise, too. Don't
hit *Delete* too quickly.

- **Watch those memorable words.** A memorable word is one
  that, well, will be remembered by a reader. These make
  writing dull. For example, if you use *pretentious* more than
  once in a few pages, people will remember it. Instead of
  repeating this memorable word, use your thesaurus. You'll
  find plenty of alternatives, like *egotistical, ostentatious,
  affected, flamboyant*. Yes, these are all memorable words,
  yet they give the same clues without being boringly
  repetitious.

  Avoid using two of the same memorable or colorful nouns,
  verbs, or adjectives in the same chapter, if possible, and
  definitely not in the same paragraph. Consider this example.

  With every move, the moonlight ricocheted off the scarlet
  sequins of her skintight nightie. The neckline nearly
  touched her waist and the skirt was slit up nearly that high,
  wasting little imagination of what was beneath it. But the
  costume's skintight invitation was wasted. Her spouse
  grunted, then hit a high-noted snore as he cuddled further in

the over-stuffed chair. A bag of cookies was nestled beneath his arm as the ESPN hockey commentator shouted that a Kings' player had nearly made a hat trick.

The images above are clear. Here's a woman who wants to attract her comatose mate's attention. But take a closer look.

Did you notice the redundancy of *nearly* and all the *wastes?* How about *skintight?* The first time the words appear they seem provocative; the second time, they are merely repetitive. Think of other images for the description of the woman's outfit. How about *body-clinging, painted-on, poured-into.* You get the picture.

We'll talk more about self-editing as we move through the book. Your job now is to watch out for word abuse when you write anything.

- **Use a thesaurus.** When I'm writing, I'll type in a word and then wonder if there's a better one for the job. I'll consider substitutes and then go back to my original choice. Sometimes, I find words this way to use for effect, as I did in the previous paragraph when I was proving my point about redundant writing.

- **Use discretion with qualifiers.** Qualifiers include such words as, *very, rather, somewhat,* and *many.* What does it really mean when we write, "He was very handsome." Is he a dazzling knockout? Or is he just a bit better than nice looking? Qualifiers dilute word meanings. Instead of using them, find the best word for the job.

- **Gender pronouns may signal an outdated writing style.** At one time it was okay to always use male gender pronouns when describing people. This sentence, for example, was considered correct: "A doctor could write any prescription he liked."

Today, the exclusive use of the male pronouns *he, his,* and *him* is considered unacceptable. However, replacing male pronouns with such phrases as, *he or she,* or *his or her,* can be awkward and wordy (this sentence is a good example of that). Smart nonfiction writers restructure the sentences. Our example sentence in the previous paragraph could be changed to, "Doctors can write any prescriptions they like." However, if you restructure a sentence to a plural form, be sure everything in the sentence "matches"; that is, if you have more than one doctor, be sure you also have plural prescriptions.

Some publishers accept alternating male and female pronouns throughout a book. However, if you aren't sure this is a house style, cover your bets by submitting a manuscript that is free of any suggestion of gender bias; carefully restructure your sentences appropriately.

Basic Punctuation Techniques You Need

Forget your fear of punctuation. Many of the rules we learned in high school have changed anyhow.

Think of punctuation this way: Punctuation marks are like road signs you see while driving. The signs are there, yet do you think about them? No. You just follow them.

When you pass a yellow sign with two children holding hands and a word that says *School*, you don't pull over to the curb, sit there for a moment, turn off the ignition, and set the brake. You don't say out loud, "Okay, this is a school zone. I have to slow to twenty miles an hour." You just do it.

The same is true for using punctuation correctly. The marks are there to direct the reader to your meaning, not to complicate your message or stop the reader.

Amateur writers abuse punctuation. They either don't know what they're doing and use it incorrectly, which muddies their meaning, or they go overboard, wildly inserting commas and apostrophes here and there. Book publishers recognize misused punctuation as a sure sign of a greenhorn who doesn't know how to write well. The publisher thinks, just how good can this beginner's book be? Don't fall into this trap when you write your book. Here's a quick and nearly painless primer of the most misused punctuation marks.

- **Period (.) .** It marks the end of a sentence. It's used after some abbreviations, such as *Dr.* and *U.S.A.* Periods appear between dollars and cents, in figures, and in e-mail addresses and websites.

- **Colon (:) .** It's used to introduce a series. (Four items were sold at the camping store: clothing, boots, sleeping bags, and camp stoves.) Colons introduce formally any material that makes a complete sentence, question, or quotation. (They talked about it all night: Which college should their pride and joy attend?) They are used in salutations (Dear Mark:) and to separate a book title from the subtitle. And colons indicate a ratio. (Mix 2 parts A with 1 part B, 2:1.)

- **Semicolon (;) .** It's used to separate clauses containing commas when too many commas would make understanding the sentence difficult. Semicolons also separate independent clauses joined by conjunctive adverbs. (The editor praised the writer's work; therefore, the book advance was enormous.)

- **Apostrophe (') .** It's used to form the possessive case of nouns and some pronouns. (The man's hat, women's clothes, each other's books, someone's notebook, somebody else's car.) Apostrophes also indicate an omission of letters in words or figures. (Can't, don't, Class of '99.)

- **Exclamation point (!) .** The exclamation point is one of the most mishandled punctuation marks in the rookie writer's toolbox. Some writers think *more* equals *better*, so rather than selecting the right words or creating images, they slap on a few exclamation points. For instance, I could write, "I remember the accident!!!!!!!!!!!" Okay, already. The reader knows I remember the accident, and the editor knows I'm not a good writer.

Read this change: The baby screamed in her car seat as the air bag exploded toward my nose, breaking my glasses against my forehead. Then the Toyota flipped once, no, twice, through the air like a toy truck. Yes, I remember the accident.

No need for any exclamation points, and you feel like you're right there.

 ## Speaking of Apostrophes

When you write the shortened, more informal version of *it is*, use *it's*. For instance, "It's time we left before it's too late."

When indicating a possessive, nongender-specific pronoun, use *its* (no apostrophe). "Its cushions were worn, and that made the easy chair more comfortable even in its old age."

If you write the contraction of *you* and *are*, the correct usage is *you're*, as in, "You're early for the conference."

Write the pronoun *your* when you want to say, "Your manuscript is flawless."

Borrowing Techniques from Fiction

Like many nonfiction book writers, I believe writing nonfiction requires more skill and cunning than writing fiction. You would probably get plenty of arguments if you threw that statement out into a group of fiction writers, but let's look at the facts.

Typically, nonfiction writers don't have beautiful protagonists (a story's leading characters). We don't have heart-melting heroes. We don't have spicy plots. We have strategies, facts, methods, statistics, formats, and knowledge. Yet we must inform and entertain our readers. We have to create page-turning work whether we're writing about door knobs or dogwood trees, diabetes or dilettantes.

That's where the craft of writing comes in. To keep the reader enthralled, we can use many of the techniques fiction writers do. Such colorful, interesting, and enjoyable writing is often called, *creative nonfiction*. Like good fiction, creative nonfiction includes the use of dialogue, distinctive adjectives, tension, characterization, and development of a theme.

Americans love to read dialogue. Dialogue also nicely breaks up your narrative, offers other opinions on a topic, allows you to quote an expert.

If you're writing a cookbook you might wonder how dialogue fits into your genre. Because we know that cookbooks today include more than recipes, you might want to quote from a famous chef or the developer of a specific cooking method. For history books, you may want to interview people who were eyewitnesses or experts in the field. With travel books, talk to locals in the area for their opinions.

Dialogue should help illustrate what the text is saying. As an example, let's say you're writing about displaced farm families. See how dialogue works here:

> The pasture stretched to the horizon, and never-ending rows of succulent corn were shimmering in the afternoon's breeze. "Farm's been in the family, mother to daughter, father to son, since the land rush of the 1870s. Had to change sometime, I guess," says Barry Clide, yanking a cap down over his sun-bronzed brow. At harvest time next summer, Clide and his kids will be out of debt for the first time in 50 years. Some people think the Clides will be rich, but their money won't be grown as corn on the family land they have tended over the years. It will come from the condominiums that will soon dot the farm landscape.

Note that the information could have been written in a straight narrative way, but hearing the farmer's own words brought out the sadness and feeling of change to life.

When writing dialogue, use more dialogue or a gesture rather than an adverb as a tag line. A *tag line* is *he said* or *she said*. For instance, the example above could have said: "Had to change sometime, I guess," says Barry Clide unconvincingly. The gesture of yanking his cap down gives a subtle image of this man's determination to make a go at the new life and a feeling of resolution that change had to come someday, yet he's not sure it's right.

Keep tag lines simple: *he said, she says, he asserted, she remarked*, all work.

Keep dialect to yourself. It's fun to write in dialect, but most readers, myself included, hate to read it. Rather, establish early on that one of the people who will be quoted has an accent, whether it's from Yonkers or the Ukraine. Your reader will get the point.

 ## Read That Manuscript Aloud

Those who write for television, the movies, and radio have a jump ahead of writers who only see their work in print. These writers read their work out loud.

Why? When you read your manuscript out loud, you can discover that some of your words are unnecessary and/or awkward, sentences are bulky or convoluted, or the final words are in rhyme. Then you can edit your work to improve its readability.

"Show, don't tell." If you've ever attended a fiction writing workshop, you've heard that advice, but it's not just for fiction writers anymore. We need it too. Readers like to make their own judgments about people and situations. If you tell everything, it's like bossing people around.

Let's say you're writing about your childhood. You could say, "We had a roasted chicken dinner after church on Sundays." Yawn. Instead, show us the color of the checkered tablecloth and the smiles of your siblings as they bowed their heads for grace. Show us Mom tucking a strand of graying hair behind her ear and the white starched apron tied around her tummy. Describe the golden bird, potatoes that rivaled cumulus clouds, and a bowl of peas that were just minutes from the garden patch.

Here's another example. You could say that John Wayne was a good actor and explain the brilliance of his roles, telling the reader every little detail. Or you could sketch out how the Duke seemed to grow taller and broader in stature every time he slapped that Stetson on his head and galloped his horse up to the camera. Then to further portray your character, combine the description with dialogue such as, "I'm just a man with a big-screen persona," said Wayne when talking to a reporter for a 1950s issue of *Variety*, "and that, Pilgrim, is an image that feels about the size of Texas when people see me in a movie."

That isn't a real quote from John Wayne. I created it for this illustration. However, notice how we get a feeling for the man from showing, instead of telling, details and facts. Again, this is a fiction technique every nonfiction writer needs to perfect.

Do add the details when you want to make a point. The details etch out the differences in the people in your book, if, in fact, you have people. Don't just say the baby had a pretty smile, say, a smile that could melt any heart. Remember to include all the senses — sight, hearing, smell, touch, taste — in your details.

Let's say you're writing a travel-adventure book, and you want to talk about a pleasant side trip readers can take to the southwest of Ireland. You'll want to give enough details to let your reader feel the atmosphere but not tell everything.

Writing about the charming pub you discovered in County Kerry, Ireland, you could say, "The bartender was a small, happy person." Ho hum. Or you could write,

> "The barkeep could have doubled for a leprechaun. That's what I thought when I asked for another beer, or that I'd had one too many already. It wasn't just his rich Gaelic accent. He played up his gnome size with breeches that just hit his knees, a white ruffled shirt, a kelly green waistcoat with oversized gold buttons, and a sly smile that said, 'Don't believe anything I say'."

Exclude details if the information isn't necessary to your book. If you go on and on about the shingles of Victorian homes in your book on architectural styles, you're going to bore everyone except those who are enamored with shingles. Of course, you can talk about roofing, but don't add details when they have nothing to contribute.

I have a friend who often says, "Absolutely correct." Everyone laughs. Written redundancies are awkward unless the person you're interviewing uses them and you're including a direct quote. In your text, steer clear of redundancies such as *personal friend*, *repeated again*, or *baby kitten.*

Planning on Illustrations? Read This First

Depending on what you're writing, sometimes you need illustrations, and sometimes it's a waste of money to hire an illustrator before the book is accepted.

Before you go to the expense of hiring an illustrator, find out what type of illustrations are expected. Are they necessary for the sale of the project? Who does the editor want to do them?

Especially with children's books, many writers think they must send finished artwork along with the manuscript. This could be a major expense that is unnecessary. Often manuscripts are sold without illustrations except for the writer's rough sketch of the art for each caption. The publisher uses a staff artist or other freelancer for the work. Save time and money and find out about the issue of illustrations as you work on your book.

Types of Nonfiction Writing

As you select the topic and begin forming the theme of your manuscript, consider the style of writing that best suits your book. As you choose the style of nonfiction, keep your reader in mind. If your topic is specialized and you're writing for an academic reader, the style in which *People* magazine is written isn't going to work.

Use a mix-and-match approach when appropriate. For instance, even writing about the most serious of topics, as I did with *What To Do When a Loved One Dies* (Dickens Press), a book about death and compassion, I blended in lighter moments, because life isn't all bad or all good.

The following are the most common contemporary nonfiction writing styles. Identify the styles of your favorite nonfiction authors by reviewing their works, and you'll learn through their examples.

- **Humor.** If you can write humor — an enviable gift — you have a powerful tool for writing nonfiction. Even if zillions of folks have told you you're funny, study material that is billed as humor and see how yours measures up.

- **Contemporary.** You'll use contractions, dialogue, descriptions, and techniques that are successful in fiction writing. Your goal is to create page-turning topics. This can be done by briefly outlining what the reader will encounter in each chapter, summarizing the material at the end of the chapter, and then describing the next informational step.

- **Academic and informational.** Your sentences may be somewhat longer. You'll be asking the reader to stick with the topic until you fully reveal the focus of your words. Here you may assume that your reader has a background in the topic, but keep in mind that publishers like to bring new readers into a genre. For instance, if you're writing a book on building a telescope, you'll probably reference some of the great telescope inventors and tell a little about them as people. This will not insult someone with an advanced degree in the subject, as long as you don't talk down to the reader.

- **Technical.** Use words that are common in the industry, but don't forget to define them the first time you put them to paper. Make sure you know exactly what the buzz words mean because you'll lose credibility if they're mangled.

Obtaining Use Permissions

Never assume you may use material that has been previously published. The original sentences writers create belong to us and have worth. However, don't be a scaredy-cat when it comes to quoting experts and people who can substantiate your premise. *Writer's Market, The Writer's Handbook,* and other writing reference books have good sections on obtaining the use of copyrighted material.

Although the copyright law says you may use a small portion of another's work without permission, the meaning of *small portion* varies according to the size and type of the work: as few as two words of a short poem is a small portion, as may be 500 words from a book of 100,000 words. Although the law doesn't lay out ironclad regulations, some publishers have their own rules of thumb for *fair use* (the correct use of copyrighted material without permission). Whether or not you need to get permission, you must always credit, or cite, all of your sources, even when you use small portions of another writer's material.

When you really need and want to get permission, you'll have to contact the original copyright holder. For example, when I wrote *For the Love of Children* (Health Communications), I wanted to use some essays that were out of print. The books in which the essays were found were no longer available, but I still had to acknowledge the copyright holder.

It's not that difficult. Check the copyright page at the front of the book or magazine, and contact the publisher. When you write the permission letter, state exactly what material you want to use. Let's say you want to quote from previous paragraphs of this book. You would contact Rodgers & Nelsen Publishing in Loveland, Colorado, and write something like this: "I'd like to have permission to excerpt from *Writing the Nonfiction Book* by Eva Shaw. I would like to use the first two paragraphs on page ____ and will give the author and publisher credit in the text." You would also need to specify what you intend to use the excerpts for by giving the title of your book, subject matter, number of pages, and publisher.

Expect to pay for the use of the material; if you don't have to, you'll be pleasantly surprised. Sometimes you have to nudge the publisher of the material to approve your request, so keep a record of your correspondence and the people you talk to.

Be sure to keep copies of the permission letter, even after you turn your manuscript over to your publisher. Things get lost, and if you relinquish your only copy of the copyright use letter, you'll be back to square one.

Manuscript Format and Preparation

Novice writers often make publishing faux pas when submitting manuscripts because they believe any creative style will be accepted. Publishing is a conservative, stuck-in-old-ways industry, so it's not surprising that the styles of submitted manuscripts are expected to match those of twenty years ago. Here are some dos and don'ts.

- **Do triple-check everything for accuracy.** Word processing programs make perfect words, but they can't tell you when the perfectly spelled *that* should instead be *hat*.

- **Don't bind manuscripts.** It's unnecessary and expensive to place the manuscript in a folder. If you have a fat manuscript, use a folding clip for the top.

- **Do give your manuscript style.** Make it clean, neat, and well written.

- **Do get it to the editor on time.**

- **Don't duplicate your manuscript on fancy paper.** But do use at least 20-pound bond. Tear off tractor-feeder edges if you use continuous paper.

- **Do double space your manuscript.** Use a font that's easy to read but not oversized. Sans Serif, Courier, and Roman are suitable in a 10 CPI (characters per inch), 12-point font. Italics, extra-fancy, and oversize fonts are not appropriate for manuscript submission. Using them may lead to rejection of even the most brilliant work.

- **Do use a font size that allows you to put 200 to 240 words on each page.**

- **Do indent paragraphs five spaces.**

 ## Writers Versus Typos

Have you ever sent a letter to a publisher, proofing it a dozen times? It's perfect. Ah, yes. The next day you read it again. Oops, oh no, golly, geez, there's a typo that's slipped in overnight. Those typos are sneaky things — at least it feels that way in my work.

Before the final printing of any cover letter, query letter, or manuscript, run it through your computer's spell-checking function one more time. I always go one step further and give it a visual proofread after the spell check. And you know what? I sometimes find errors that could be embarrassing. To help you remember that word-processing programs produce perfect words but not perfect logic, here's a little poem:

My Spell Checker
(Author unknown)

I have a little spell checker.
It came with my PC.
It plainly marks for my revue,
mistakes I cannot sea
I've run this poem threw it,
I'm sure your please too no.
It's letter perfect and its write,
My checker tolled me sew.

* **Don't insert extra lines between paragraphs.**

* **Don't justify your right margin.** This changes the word count on the page.

* **Do leave about three to four inches at the top of the page as you begin each chapter.**

* **Don't cheat on margins.** Top, bottom, right, and left margins should all be about one inch. But if you've received another directive from your editor on layout, by all means follow the instructions.

* **Do make your cover letter clear, to the point, and grammatically correct.** If you're sending the manuscript on *speculation* (without any promises from the agent or publisher), include sufficient postage for the return of your manuscript, or note in your letter not to return it. That's smart because regardless of how careful the postal system is, it will look shopworn. If you don't want the manuscript back, include a letter-size SASE (self-addressed stamped envelope) with your submission so that the editor or agent can let you know the status of the manuscript.

* **Do add extra touches.** I like to use blue paper clips that match the colored ink used to print my name and address on my stationery. A very successful, self-promoting writer I know uses gold-colored paper clips. These additions are tasteful and catch an editor's eye.

Smart Ways to Prepare to Write

You've done your homework. You've researched the topic so that you feel confident. You know how you would like to handle the book. Your next step is to begin preparation.

Unless you're already an expert on the topic, it's past time to read everything available on your subject. Immediately go to the library and make fast friends with the reference librarians. They love to help serious writers.

Take another trip to a large bookstore and purchase books on the same topic you'll be writing about. It might be wise to build a budget. Keep all your receipts. These verify tax deductions for your tax return.

Some writers refuse to read the competition for fear of subconsciously plagiarizing it. However, by reading other books on your subject, you can see how and where they fall short on information. You can make your book even better or give it a slightly different slant or marketing hook. Also, check the references cited in these other books. They could lead you to some little-known sources of information.

Keep a list of all your reference or background sources, or photocopy the cover and copyright page of all books and articles used. Include information on how to locate them again.

If you have any doubt about needing a book or article as a reference when you're writing, or for future articles or books, keep some type of record — on your computer, in a card file, on a note at the end of your copy of the query. I'm a low-tech person, so I often photocopy the copyright page of the book and write the library catalogue number directly on the same sheet.

Finish the Paragraph

Select one of the partial sentences below and finish it. If you like, you can go down the list and have a writing exercise every day for a week.

Many of those who have tried this exercise find that they feel free to blend fiction with their own thoughts. Keep the messages light or become serious. No one is looking over your shoulder.

The only rule is that you must write at least 100 words or for five minutes, whichever is more.

1. When the holidays arrive, I become ...

2. Mary had had it with Bob, so when she ...

3. Today's politicians could take a lesson from ...

4. Eating in a fast-food restaurant is much like ...

5. If Susan B. Anthony were alive today, she would say ...

6. For a bibliophile, there is no better place than ...

7. At my age, I should have been more leery of ...

CHAPTER 4

Researching Made Manageable

To affect the quality of the day,
that is the highest of arts.
— Henry David Thoreau

Do you love or hate doing research? Few writers stand in the middle of the road on this issue. Personally, I'm on the hate side. However, I also know that I cannot write well or have any depth to my writing unless I knuckle under and research. So I've learned plenty of tricks to make it almost easy or at least manageable.

In this chapter we'll cover how and why you need to streamline the research process, how to design a workable research plan, and how to make fact-finding easy. Primary research tips and the use of high-tech helpers will also play a role.

Forget that old stereotype about the tedium of research. Research can be nearly pain free once you know the tricks of the trade.

Streamlining the Research Process

Once you start looking into a topic to write about, one thing leads to another. Most of the time this is great — you're finding a path to the answers. The flip side, however, is that many writers get lost in the discussion or research process.

The first and only rule of research is: Stay focused.

Researching a topic or many topics for a book can be frustrating. It can be fun. Most of all it takes time that isn't actual writing time. As you focus on your current book project, think first about how much information you need and the type of information you're striving for.

1. **Decide *generally* what your topic will be.** Don't hesitate to jot down other possibilities.

2. **Survey the literature of your field.** Make sure you understand unfamiliar terms.

3. **Decide if you will use primary or secondary sources.** Primary research is the firsthand stuff, like surveys, questionnaires, and interviews. Secondary research is material you've collected from published sources, including books, newspapers, magazines, and the Internet.

4. **Decide how much material you will need.** Typically, you'll need more than you think you will.

5. **Decide what level of authority you'll need to consult.** Scholarly? Popular?

6. **Budget your time.**

7. **Decide on the types of reference tools you'll need.** Bibliographies? Encyclopedias? Abstracts? Diaries? Newspaper articles? Will you locate them at the library or on the Internet?

8. **Ask for assistance from others who may have information.** If you still hit a brick wall, ask people, "Where might I find more information?" Most likely someone will give you hints to move you on to the next step.

9. **Become Mr./Ms. Sherlock Holmes.** The facts are out there; you just have to find the clues to put the whole story together.

10. **If you simply can't find enough information, you still have choices.** (a) Go back to the beginning and start with another topic. Or (b) search deeper because you've discovered an area that hasn't been exploited by another writer.

Let the Experts Come to You

So you need to talk with someone who is an authority on the Crimean War? The eating habits of grizzly bears? The best plants for low-maintenance gardens?

You can find knowledgeable people by looking in a research book that is right in your own home. And you don't have to pay a dime to use it. It's the phone company's Yellow Pages.

People who are in a specific business are experts, whether they are carpet layers or cake decorators. (See Chapter 8 for information on how to interview and get the scoop from experts.) To find that expert on the Crimean War, check the Yellow Pages for the nearest college or university, and track down a professor who specializes in European history. To find an expert on the eating habits of grizzly bears, look under Animal Trainers or Zoo or the National Park Service. And to get information on low-maintenance gardens, refer to the listings for landscape architects, landscape services, or garden centers. You get the idea.

11. **Build your bibliography now.** As you collect and use material you've researched, add each citation to a bibliography for your book. Even if you decide later not to include a bibliography with the finished manuscript, the

bibliography will help you to refocus should you need to return to the original research. I do this by creating a new page at the very end of the manuscript or starting a new computer file with the information. I list all the information necessary for a complete bibliographic citation, just as in any book. When I've finished writing the book, the bibliography is complete. I don't need to spend time searching for a publisher's name or copyright date for any of the work I have used in my research.

There are no guarantees your research will go smoothly, that the facts and figures you'll find will increase the marketability of your book, or that the material will boost the book's authenticity. However, you can increase the chances of success if, when you *think* you've finished all your research, you stop and ask yourself the following questions.

- **How is my background information?** Do I fully understand this topic? From the material I've reviewed, could I intelligently talk about it and write about it? To add sparkle to your writing, include little-known facts; this separates your work from slipshod writers.

- **Do I understand all the terms that are discussed in the research?** Can I define them so my reader can also understand them? Are buzz words defined? Even if you have a basic understanding of the meaning of a word or phrase, it is helpful to your reader to have a precise definition. Everyone knows what an *attitude* is, but psychologists have a very precise definition in mind when they use the word. A specialized dictionary, available for nearly every field, can help you nail down a term.

- **Have I fully explored the context of my topic?** Even the most current topic will have some history or background. Look at the people and places involved, review the issues, think about the effect your topic will have on the future. Remember, an older version of an encyclopedia or other reference book might very well provide you with information that can be cross-referenced to the details you need.

* **Have I included the most recent information on my established topic?** Have I provided enough current information to make my topic relevant to the contemporary reader?

* **Have I objectively considered every side of the issue?** Even in position papers it pays to understand and be able to articulate both sides of the issue. Consider the advantages of keeping the perspective as broad as possible when completing your research.

* **Have I obtained information from as many appropriate sources as possible?** Many writers don't consider any research beyond books, magazines, journals, newspapers, and the electronic media. Large libraries and specialized libraries have collections that include historical documents, diaries, statistics, maps, charts, graphs, letters, manuscripts, and photographs. These sources are invaluable and can add depth to your writing.

For example, if I'm writing a book about gold rush towns in early California, I could write about how hard life was for the workers. Or I could include the words quoted from a personal diary of a gold miner who actually suffered the hardships.

* **Have I analyzed the quality of my research material?** Is the author of the book I'm quoting from biased or known as the expert in the field? Is the publishing firm owned by a political organization or nonprofit group? Are the facts reliable? Have I checked the information against other sources to verify the reliability?

As an illustration, let's say you're writing a book about surrogate motherhood. You can research information in a variety of places from the *New York Times* to the *National Enquirer*. Select research that is available from a reliable, authoritative source if that's the information you want to produce.

- **Have you found most of the material you hope to have on the topic?** Have you asked a reference librarian about other possible sources? Have you talked with experts in the discipline and asked for their recommendations?

When you have finished researching everything you believe possible, take time to review all the information, organize it in an easy-to-use manner, and then go back to the library for a quick review.

Make a Plan, Work the Plan

A thesis statement written early in your research focuses *your* attention, not the reader's. It's okay to modify your statement or even radically change it. Your thesis statement is a compass that guides you through the maze of your work.

Many nonfiction writers strive to narrow their thesis statements to 25 words or fewer, a mere sound bite of information, a blurb, a solid idea, call it what you will. When creating a thesis statement for this book, I might have written: *Writing the Nonfiction Book* teaches how to research, format, write, and sell a nonfiction book.

The book you're holding tells how to organize material, outline, interview, compose sentences, target readers, and then write a nonfiction book. It talks about working with agents and publishers, getting the most from writers' conferences, and even extending the shelf life of your book. It follows the thesis statement above.

A thesis statement about your book helps you focus. You can return to it often to make sure you're on track. The following examples show how to develop a thesis statement from a broad, general idea. Each step shows a further narrowing of the topic in order to ultimately arrive at a legitimate thesis statement.

Keeping Your Word

Look over the writer's contract below. It's designed for you. When you know you've done as much as you can, sign and date it. Duplicate this sheet and use it for each idea and book project.

☐ 1. I have read what other writers have written on my topic. I have checked *Books in Print* and other sources for information.

☐ 2. I have developed and researched the topic with one or two specific publishers in mind. I know I may want to broaden the search, but I have targeted the first two publishers.

☐ 3. I have decided on a specific aspect of my subject. I know what publishers will use this type of topic and the slant they require to buy the material.

☐ 4. I have asked myself questions about the specific slant including: What type of nonfiction book will I propose to write — how-to, self-help, informational, historical, humorous, etc.

☐ 5. I know exactly what I can offer the publisher that other writers can't . . .why I am the best writer, or the only writer, for this topic and why my concept is unique.

☐ 6. I have written a query letter that sells my slant and my special writing abilities. The query includes the flavor of my topic and information that will help the publisher decide to give me the contract.

☐ 7. I have produced and proofread my query. It is perfect. I've kept a copy of the query and included a list of those publishers I've sent it to. The information is on disk or in my query file.

☐ 8. I have included a SASE with the query.

☐ 9. I will continue writing queries on other topics until I hear from the publishers.

☐ 10. When I hear that the publisher likes my book idea and a contract is negotiated, I will write the book to the publisher's specifications.

☐ 11. If my book idea is rejected, I will immediately locate a new market for the topic or re-adjust the topic to capture another publisher's interest.

☐ 12. I mail out at least one query letter each day.

_____   _____
              Author   Date

Broad ◄────────────────────────────► Narrow

Mark Twain——*The Adventures of Huckleberry Finn*——
Significance of ending
THESIS: Huck's departure at the end of the novel reflects
Twain's own dissatisfaction with civilization.

Broad ◄────────────────────────────► Narrow

Public Schools——Length of school——Effect of extended
year
THESIS: An extended school year has positive effects on
learning, student attitudes toward school, and the retention of
skills from year to year.

A thesis statement *should* be:
* A complete sentence summarizing the point of view of your
  book.
* A specific declaration of your main idea.
* A statement reflecting your position.

A thesis statement should *not* be:
* A topic or subject by itself. That information tells what the
  book is about, not what you and your research have to say
  about the matter.
* A question. Because it is not a statement, a question implies
  that an answer will follow.
* A general statement that lacks a detailed point of view. A
  general statement may give background information but it
  doesn't reflect your point of view. Here's an example of a
  statement that's too general to be used as a thesis statement:
  Children younger than one year of age are not physically
  mature enough to begin toilet training.

Fact-Finding Made Easier

Once you have a thesis statement, finding facts will be less
painful.

There are a number of good books for writers on how to research. My favorite is *Find It Fast: How to Uncover Expert Information on Any Subject* by Robert L. Berman (Harper & Row). Berman continues to update the book, so look for the newest edition. Berman and I agree that obvious sources are often the best. The library right in your hometown or one accessed via the Internet can always serve you well for research.

Start with the basic and worthy encyclopedia. Some new writers think that they are far too intelligent to use an encyclopedia for research. And maybe they are, but I keep a set of Funk & Wagnalls, purchased at a library book sale for $16, within reaching distance. Yes, I've heard it all: "Books? Why don't you use a CD-ROM or find it on the Web?" I do have a CD-ROM, and I can mosey my way around cyberspace, but facts are facts. Most historical ones are right in my tattered set of encyclopedias. It's often easier to lean across my desk and snatch up a volume than to move from one program or website to another.

This was brought home recently when I was beginning research on a book about people who have overcome great obstacles and succeeded. I wanted to compare a feat of daring to climbing Mt. Everest. Now, I could have gone into the Internet and most likely clicked on www.MtEverest.com or something like it. I could have slipped in the CD-ROM encyclopedia that came with my computer. But I just wanted to know how big that mountain is. In about 30 seconds, Volume E of my Funk & Wagnalls informed me of the height (29,028 feet, 8,848 meters); the first noteworthy expedition (1922); and the mountain's exact location (one of the peaks of the Himalayas on the frontier of Nepal). Yes, electronic information is fast, but let your fingers do some work too.

The moral here is that facts are facts. Fond du Lac is still in Wisconsin. Stephen Foster still wrote "Camptown Races," and the ancient poet Firdawsi (c. 935 – c. 1020) is still known as the Homer of Persia. Get those facts however you can.

Work the plan that's beginning to gel, and as you research, consider various avenues. You'll want to consult books, magazines, government documents, pamphlets, theses and dissertations, annual reports, bibliographies, who's who books, and guides to literature.

Your best research information comes from primary sources — firsthand accounts. You'll find primary research can be developed from questionnaires, interviews, observations, personal experiences, and experiments. Secondary sources are materials that have been interpreted or collected by another person and included in articles, books, and speeches. Be aware that you may find primary information within secondary information in the form of direct quotes from experts and eye-witness observers.

Get Yourself in That Primary Picture

Research from books and information from experts adds depth to your nonfiction book. Good writers take research further and experience exactly what they're writing about.

For a moment pretend you're writing a book on carving traditional Native American canoes. It's fine and dandy to watch someone do the carving, sweat over a particularly tricky design, only to have a chunk of wood break off and ruin months of work. It's another story when you've actually struggled with a chisel and felt how the blisters, the dreams, and the feelings of accomplishment form as a log turns into a boat. One mistake and your piece of art could be ruined. You may never finish the canoe or even make a straight cut with a chisel, but there will be more wisdom in your words if you directly experience your subject.

You do not have to be an expert to write on an expert subject. You do have to know how to ask questions, learn as you go, and translate the information into the written word.

Save Money When Traveling

Researching your book may require you to travel to the source expert, home, or origin of your topic. Remember the following trip tips.

Ask for press discounts when booking hotel, car, and airline reservations. You might be charged less. (It helps if you belong to one of the national writers' associations and have a press card.)

Never tell anyone that you're new in town. Tell people you come down this way all the time. Those travelers who say they know little of the city are the easiest marks. Do so and you may end up traveling five extra miles to get across a two-mile town.

Pretend you know something about where you are, and then if you feel you're being ripped off, overcharged, or underserved, speak up.

Ask for receipts, including those for using a toll road, parking, and taxicabs. Keep all your receipts; they are essential for tax deductions.

High-Tech Helps

Today I merrily maneuver down the information superhighway, but those who have known me for a while realize that wasn't always true. I'm a low-tech kinda' gal coming from the days of manual typewriters. Okay, I admit it. I fought the conversion to computers and I fought the Internet. Then one day a woman in one of my classes produced a technological argument that I couldn't win. She said, "The Internet is like indoor plumbing. Once you get used to it, everything else will seems old-fashioned."

If you're still unsure about how technology can help, take some community college classes or get a simple book on using the newest computer software. Get hooked up to a server and learn to use the Internet. The time you save using e-mail alone will be worth a mint.

I was reminded of how technology saves time and money just recently. As I was working on this book, I was also putting the finishing touches on a travel and relocation book called *The Insiders' Guide to San Diego*, from Falcon Press/ Insiders' Guides. It's a big book, more than 200,000 words, and never once did I touch a piece of paper throughout the project. All editing was done online, so I didn't have to print out the manuscript. I sent all chapters to my editor across the country via e-mail. Never once did I have to pay postage or express mail charges or even find an envelope. Had this been a little book with few changes and deadlines, these costs might have been insignificant. But *The Insiders' Guide* has more than 30 chapters, which would have meant 30 trips to the post office and 30 times to have to stand in line. I can do the numbers on this one, and even with the cost of an Internet service, I'm ahead in time and money.

Working on this book with Rodgers & Nelsen, I stay in e-mail touch every day, sometimes many times a day, with the publisher and editor. I send e-mail proposals to my agent for her first review. I contact public relations people and magazines by e-mail. If this low-tech person can do it, you have no excuses.

All the high-tech helpers from laptops to electronic notebooks to daytimers can seem complicated, but they don't need to be. Talk to other writers and people you respect, who know their way around cyberspace. Find out from them about software, servers, and information that will help you with your needs. Estimate how to get the most out of the Internet and decide at what level you're comfortable.

Using the Internet for research is a constructive tool, yet it comes with drawbacks. You see, anyone who can create a website can assume the role of an expert, an authority, or a business guru. Perverted as it might seem, there are folks who create worthless but authentic-appearing material just for the fun of tricking you and me.

When using the Internet's capabilities for research, you'll have to discern the quality, suitability, original sources, and authenticity of the material. The caution? Don't believe everything you read, whether it arrives electronically or in print. Here are some tips for evaluating sources.

Consider the depth and scope of an Internet source to decide how complete the coverage is. Has the author listed all sources or only favorite sources? Are the major areas covered or are only a smattering of sources included?

Where did the material originate? Are there any facts, statistics, or quotes attributed to another source that are verifiable? If the sources are not verifiable, is the source worth using? Internet sources provided by government agencies, leading nonprofit organizations, and universities are usually higher in quality, but it pays to be suspicious. As anyone who has ever watched political commercials during a pre-election mud-slinging contest will affirm, numbers and facts can be manipulated.

The degree of quality material is tough to assess unless you're already an expert on the topic. Look for clues such as typos, grammar errors, or suspicious connections with other sources. If experts at companies and faculty members at universities are willing to put their names on material, it assures the researcher of some degree of quality.

It would seem that anything posted on the Internet would be up-to-the-minute. Not so. Sometimes material stays on the Internet because it has been forgotten. Unlike books, which have the copyright date in the front, it's difficult to tell when some citations or sources were created or updated on the Web. Check for publication date, date of last update, and cross-referencing to other material that is current.

Once you find the sources and decide to include the expert information, quotes, or other material, you'll need to give credit to the author just as you would if you found the data in a book. This is done through citations.

Let's get something straight: Unless you're writing a dissertation, a journal article, or a paper for an academic application, forget about footnotes. They're dead. But citations, included in your text or, if you must, as end notes, are a way of acknowledging sources of information. Citations also provide a path to trace the source of your material so a reader can learn more on your topic.

Although there is no current, perfect way to cite an Internet source, be sure to include the following:

* Author. This may be a department, university, or organization.
* Date of publication. If you're citing an e-mail message or Usenet newsgroup posting, use the date on the message or posting.
* Title of the resource. The title may be in the posted message or website.
* The location of the research on the Internet. Include the type of Internet resource — e-mail, URL, etc..

Here are examples of citations of Internet information:

Winter, Mark. (1999) *WebLinks* [World Wide Web]. Available: http://www.weblinks.ac.uk/uni/academic/A-C/ chem/web-elements/web-elements-home.html

National Association of Press Photographers. (1999, August 12) *National Press Photographers Association* [World Wide Web]. Available: http:// www.sunsite.unc.edu/nppa

Here's an example of an electronic source citation:

Wood, Daniel B., "Largest Welfare-to-Work Program Called a Success," *The Christian Science Monitor*, April 20, 1999, 3. CD NewsBank, NewsBank, Inc.

Why go through all the research, low-tech or high-tech versions? Why document your sources? Why get permission to use previously published material? To save your butt.

Once in a while we read in the newspaper or hear about a leading writer or media person who manipulates or distorts some facts, quotations, or statistics. The resulting exposé is ugly and disgraceful. Sure, we've all felt temptation's pull to

modify a fact or a statistic to prove a point. However, if just
one reader discovers the truth, contacts your book publisher,
who then contacts you, your credibility is in the dumpster.

 ## Avoid Software Nightmares

"Hey, you there. Wanna copy of this great
new program? A writer like you should save
some money. Half the original price, and it's
yours."

Well-meaning friends, computer gurus, and a slew of
others are out there to tempt you. *However*, buying or
using unauthorized, pirated copies of software is not only
illegal, it's potentially fatal to your career. Consider the
viruses lurking in computer programs these days. You
may be able to save $100 or more by buying pirated
software, but if your computer crashes or munches your
book because of a glitch, the savings are insignificant.
Buying an unauthorized copy or borrowing a friend's
software is like another writer or an editor using your
latest manuscript without paying you a cent. It's stealing.

When you buy an original copy, you get the manuals,
store assistance, and most likely a toll-free telephone
number for technical support. At the other end of your
phone is a friendly computer wizard ready to serve you.
For those of us who are only marginally computer literate,
that's well worth the cost.

I always tell my classes, when I reach this point in the
semester, about the inkling I have that there's a persnickety
retired high school principal in Big River, Maine. The
principal reads everything I produce (as well as everything you
write too) and can't wait to find a screw-up. Of course, this
individual isn't real, but if we ever step over the line by
altering information or stretching the truth, there's probably
somebody out there somewhere who will call us on the carpet.

Write a Mini-Story

Try this simple, inspirational, and challenging exercise. Close your eyes and run your finger up and down the columns below. Let it stop wherever and whenever it chooses. Look at the four words on the line of the word you selected.

Use those four words to write a mini-story of about 100 words or more. The only rule is you must use the first word in the group (the word closest to the left margin) in your first sentence. Put the remaining words in as they fit.

Like our other creative aerobic exercises, this one gets you over the "white page jitters." It gets your energy up to tackle the real work of writing your book. With all the possibilities below, you'll have enough exercise for quite some time.

lemon	rock	shipwreck	vacuum cleaner
trapped	terrier	juice	sandwich
pie	yellow	volunteer	tornado
pencil	taboo	mustard	truck
loved	odor	feast	silver
explorer	father	frenzy	ants
balmy	sink	native	zipper
waterfall	red	cruise	crystal
wine	kittens	button	chocolate
dust	mountain	computer	treasure
wood	grapes	candle	apples
flag	Paris	monkey	rope
quicksand	sneeze	dessert	breeze
fire	truck	lace	song
trout	serious	dictionary	pork
shells	videos	tuna fish	unemployment
garlic	Florida	hot pink	bananas
dinosaur	crow	daisy	hug

CHAPTER 5

The Specifics of the Nonfiction Genres

*Most of the material a writer works with
is acquired before the age of fifteen.*
— Willa Cather

We often hear about genres from those who write fiction.
Genre (pronounced *zhänrə*) means a category of artistic work
that has a particular form, content, technique, or the like.
Fiction writers talk about the genre of mysteries (and the
subgenres of police procedurals and "cozies," those Agatha
Christie-style murder mysteries), the genre of romances (with
lots of subsets here too), and on to science fiction (techno to
fantasy), horror, and experimental fiction.

What does *genre* mean to nonfiction writers? Plenty. Try
books that share courage or morals, memoirs of business
leaders and pioneers, computer books, cookbooks, science
books, humor books, and the ever popular how-to books, with
self-help books following close behind.

Nonfiction book writing includes not only specific genres,
but also subsets, or subgenres. For instance, in the humor
genre, you can have G-rated books and raunchy ones. If
you're creating a cookbook, you might want to write a book
filled exclusively with recipes or one that intertwines a story or
travel adventure with descriptions of meals.

In this chapter you'll find out how to format the main genres and where to discover more information about subgenres.

How to Find *Your* Place on the Bookstore Shelf

"Do your homework."

Can't you just hear a teacher or parent saying that? Now you're hearing it again, and this time you had better listen if you want to be a nonfiction book writer.

To be successful at writing nonfiction, you must research the genre in which you plan to place your book. This gives you the insider's scoop on what readers and publishers want. To accomplish this, you'll have to read what's out there, and then evaluate why some books sparked your interest and why some didn't. This important step prevents you from unknowingly duplicating a format that doesn't work.

Although you'll want to avoid following a formula as you write your book, you should be sure to include what the reader expects to see. For example, instructions must appear in a how-to book, steps should show up in a self-help manual, and the personal saga needs to have an earth-shaking climax, as the memoir on overcoming espresso abuse culminates in your main character walking away from a triple latte.

Your book needs to have a category in which to fit, a place waiting on the bookstore shelf. Yes, once in a while a book comes along that doesn't fit any category. However, if this is your first nonfiction book-writing adventure, it makes sense to write a book that matches one of the established areas.

You can identify the niche your book fits into by taking your field trip to a big bookstore, as we discussed in Chapter 2. Walk up and down the aisles. Stop and look at the books situated in your genre. Read some of the books by your competitors. Remember, the books you see were once just sparks of ideas, just like the spark you have now. The difference, of course, is that the author wrote the book, sold it to a publisher, and the publisher printed and distributed it.

Take a notebook with you and, as you browse the shelves,

jot down details you like about the books in your genre. For instance:

- Do you prefer to read a chapter preview at the beginning of each chapter and then a summary at the end?

- Do you like to have quotes mixed in with the text?

- How do you feel about sidebar or boxed information, as is found in this guide?

Some of what you'll notice in a book is design. For instance, the icons that pull your eye to important tips here in this book were the book designer's brainchild. The font choice, page layout, and even illustrations are design issues. When your book has found a home with a publisher, you may be asked for your opinion on design issues, but don't count on it. Planning the cover and internal design of a book is an art form best left to professionals.

After the bookstore field trip, return to your hometown library and meander through some of the less current books in your genre. See how they are written. Let's say you're writing a sports fitness book. Do you like the ones with graphs, charts, and statistics? How about those that have fill-in logs to track progress?

Wait. You're not finished yet. If either you or the library has copies, review back issues of *Publisher's Weekly*, specifically the seasonal issues. Book selling, like fashion, has seasons — winter, spring, summer, and fall. Read the reviews for those books that *Publisher's Weekly* recommends and find out why. If a *Publisher's Weekly* reviewer praises the clear steps in a how-to book, get a copy of that book and see how the material has been presented. Again, take some notes because this information will help you make your book a quick sell.

You can learn a lot from other books in your field. Use this information to launch your book as the special text it is.

Economize on Writers' Magazines

Save a bundle on magazines by sharing subscriptions with other writers. Do it by splitting the initial costs or by each member of the group subscribing to a different magazine.

To make this system work, set up some ground rules so everyone knows what is expected.

This is how I've done it. Three of my writing friends and I have all, at one time or another, wanted to subscribe to *Publisher's Weekly*. At nearly $120 a year, it's pricey. However, by splitting the cost four ways, the cost becomes reasonable. When the magazine arrives at Lee's mailbox, a routing slip (like those used in an office) is attached to the cover. Lee has three days to read the magazine, then it's passed on to Chris, and then on at the same speed until everyone has seen the copy. No one is allowed to tear anything out until that issue has made its rounds. We photocopy any information we're interested in.

Should one of us want the magazine back, we indicate that on the routing slip. No takers? It's donated to the library, a writing class, or tossed into the recycling bin — whatever is appropriate. We also share subscriptions to other writers' magazines.

How much money can be saved? With *Publisher's Weekly* alone, we each saved more than $75.00 this year. In addition, we subscribe together to *Writer's Digest*, *The Writer*, *Book Marketing Update*, and *Poets & Writers*, so we have saved even more money. If you and other writers want to keep up on issues found in women's, sports, or travel publications, start sharing those subscriptions too.

When only two people share a magazine, fold under the top corner of the cover if you want the magazine back after your friend has reviewed it. With no corner turned under, your friend need not return it.

How-To Books

Let's say you're writing a book on how to make baskets from natural materials that can be found in forests. You're an expert and have years of experience in the basket-making field.

If you jump right into the basket projects without telling your reader about the types of plants and fibers that are best for making baskets, or the tools necessary to turn pine needles into baskets, the reader will not be successful with the projects. To be truthful, it's doubtful that you'll get to first base with a publisher.

How-to books, the biggest selling nonfiction genre, are filled with instructions, information, tips, suggestions, examples, and illustrations. That's what you need to include if you want to sell in this field.

Instructions must be geared to your reader's level of understanding. A few years ago I collaborated on *50 Wooden Crafts to Make with Kids* (Crown/Random House). The crafts were designed for children to make, but parents had to help. Instructions were written simply enough so that both kids and parents could successfully complete the projects, but neither felt put off by the language. Write for both the sophisticated and the novice in the field, unless, of course, your book is for experts only.

Instructions and information must be sequential. You can't jump around with advice, or the reader just won't get it. Map out an order for the logical division of information and follow it. This may sound far too simple, but basic works. Look at the cooking instructions on a can of condensed soup. The instructions begin, "In a medium sauce pan . . ." They don't say, "Cook soup over medium heat until hot." Some beginning soup makers might misconstrue these directions to mean that they cook the unopened can right on the stove — a bad idea. As you're working up your subject's instructions and information, keep soup in mind.

Give examples to help readers understand your theories or the text. The soup illustration above is an example that's easy to understand and visualize. Depending on your topic, you may have case studies, interviews, endorsements, or accounts, or you may want to explain more about the project or system. You may want to share some of your own opinions and experiences as I have sprinkled through this how-to book.

Every chapter should support your total concept and eventually conclude with what you set out to achieve. If you're writing a book on how to wallpaper your home, you'll probably give the how-to information right off and then go on to give additional recommendations for special areas, problems the wallpaperer will encounter, and designer application techniques. As your readers move through the beginning techniques, they will finally become proficient enough to do the specialty methods you recommend later. Present your information sequentially.

Self-Help Books

Books that suggest how to change life patterns, from having more attractive fingernails to moving through the stages of grief, are self-help books. Americans consume them like chocolates. Smart writers do well selling this genre.

The keys to formulating self-help books are similar to the ways how-to books are put together. You must provide sound information in a sequential format. As the name of the genre indicates, self-help books tell people how to improve themselves. Traditionally, self-help books are heavier with examples than how-to books and speak to readers as if they were old friends. They'll often have case studies, or true stories, of individuals overcoming great odds and finding success using the self-help program described in the book.

Authors of self-help books may be medical doctors or psychologists or movie stars or regular folks like you and me. The self-help genre includes trendy books written by gurus that seem destined to top the bestseller list. It includes celebrities who tout their newest twelve-step recovery plan or fitness program that promises to make our bodies as beautiful as theirs. And don't forget books by therapists, which give help to all sorts of dysfunctional people.

A few years ago I consulted with a writer who wanted to move from writing for magazines, although he was making a good living doing so, to the book field. He was working on an inspirational topic. I'll call him "Ted."

Ted had what he hoped was a knockout proposal. The agent sent it to five or six publishers. There were no positive responses and not even one personal rejection letter with something like, "Good writing, but can't use it." Ever the optimist, Ted didn't know he was in trouble. The agent mentioned changing the focus, but Ted either didn't understand or didn't want to hear that advice. When we met at a writers' conference he asked me to take a look at his proposal and added, "I just can't see where I'm missing the mark."

Ted's writing was good and I liked the way he presented his emotional story. The book was entertaining, and if I were temporarily out of all other reading material, I would have zoomed right through it. The problem was that he only talked about how the topic affected him. It was a "me" book.

If Ted had been a movie star, a member of the president's cabinet, or a sports hero, rather than a guy who works for a Seattle computer company, the book would have sold. As it was, he needed more. Ted was going to have to tell people the steps he went through to discover this inner wisdom. He needed to turn it into a self-help book instead of a memoir or collection of ramblings about the secrets of life.

This story has a happy ending. Ted went back to the keyboard and developed a twelve-step plan leading to a clear understanding of his topic. He changed the format of the book to include his advice to readers on how to make similar changes in their lives. He gave the proposal and the manuscript back to the agent, and it sold to the next publisher who looked at it.

Unlike the publishing market of the past, today you need to be an expert to write and sell a self-help book. However, the expert doesn't have to be someone with three Ph.D.s, but rather it can be someone who is a bona fide authority. Here's where the rest of us get into the picture so we too can write self-help books and get endorsements from academic experts or medical professionals. If you have the background and experience to write a self-help book but lack the formal educational credentials, your first step might be to connect with someone who has the degrees. Be sure to read the section on Finding Experts and Using Quotes in Chapter 8 for ways to add credibility to any self-help book.

Writing as a Team Occupation

In the "two heads are better than one" category, working with a writing partner can double your income. How so? If your partner is strong on grammar and composition, and your strengths lie in interviewing and dialogue, you may have a match made in bestseller heaven.

Select a partner with care. You must both have similar dedication, work habits, time for the project, and goals.

Writing with a partner also works well if one of you is the writer and the other a legitimate expert. For example, you might write with a doctor who researches cures for cancer or a financial whiz who is the president of an investment firm. While these individuals may or may not write well enough, a writer of your caliber will be able to get a message out and make some money for both of you. Your writing career will get a boost too.

Formalize your relationship with a good written contract.

Biographies and Autobiographies

As you mingle with writers, you're going to find those who scoff at the fact that you're thinking of writing a biography or your autobiography. "They never sell." "Boring." "No longer fashionable." Your answer can be a flat-out, pshaw.

Granted they aren't as easy to sell to a publisher as how-to and self-help books, but there's always a market for personal accounts. Doris Kearns Goodwin, a historian, made the *New York Times* bestseller list with a coming-of-age, love-of-baseball autobiography in *Wait Till Next Year* (Simon and Schuster). She was also honored with a Pulitzer Prize for another Simon and Schuster book, *No Ordinary Time*, a biography of Franklin and Eleanor Roosevelt. When you think of autobiographies, remember *The Diary of Anne Frank*.

The key to selling anything, especially biographies and autobiographies, is excellent writing. The book must be thoroughly investigated, all facts correct, and written in a storyteller's hand. If you're serious about putting a life down on paper, whether it's yours, or a historical or celebrity figure, learn to research and use the analysis tools available to writers. Keep in mind that even ordinary people do extraordinary things.

If you're writing a biography or autobiography, you needn't start in the beginning of your subject's life, as in, "I was born in . . ." That approach is considered dull. Rather, think of the drama, the heartache, the humor, the inspirational incidents of the life you're describing. Start your book at a point of tension in your subject's life: When she is being sentenced to prison for attempting to kill her abusive ex-spouse, when the storm is brewing over the Rockies and he has lost the trail, when your subject awakens and realizes her vision is blurred so badly she can't see the baby's features. Pull at our heart strings — enlist all the creative tricks that fiction writers use to make us care.

Recently I helped a retired school principal compose and edit the saga of his family who overcame great odds to immigrate to America. The great odds included escaping from Nazi tyranny, Communism's iron hand, and countless instances of near death, disease, and starvation. When the family finally arrived in San Francisco, the story unfolds, they were not allowed entry for they had no country of origin. This happened because they had been running for their lives for years.

Here was a supposed amateur writer, although he certainly was not amateurish in his way with words, brewing up stories he had heard from his father. I nearly cried — for joy — as I read his story because he got me to care about people and places I'd never known and times I can only imagine. He did it with simple language and images that were as sharp as the dagger of a Nazi thug.

I already knew that the family had made it to safety and settled in America. How? The writer was born in Fresno, California, so the family obviously had survived. But the tension and the tales of the heroic man, his young wife, and their brave children affected me so much I couldn't wait to turn the pages. That's tension. That's drama. That's compelling writing.

Common Sense and Hard Work Take the Prize

Don't be intimidated by the super creative people, including those with scores of degrees, who produce three-dimensional images with phrases that make you seesaw between a guffaw and your heart ripping to shreds. Or have the ability to whip out a nail-biting saga of good versus evil in the time it takes you to jot down a grocery list.

In the writing classes I've attended, and some at which I've spoken, I've met them — the truly creative writers who can't seem to finish a piece of writing, let alone market their work. I envy their ability to capture golden words that go from mind to paper. In the big picture of life, though, the writers who make it are those who are disciplined, meet deadlines, sell their work, and continue to write, often in the face of rejection. The ultra-artistic types, on the whole, seem to stumble as they cross the fifty-yard line while we're standing next to the goal post.

Talent is great, yet stick-to-it-ness brings home the bucks.

Not everyone who writes a biography or autobiography plans to show it to an agent or sell it to a publisher. Actually, in my writing classes, a common scenario is for students to feel compelled to write their life stories or, as in the case above, to write their families' stories for posterity. If this is the type of nonfiction book that's tickling your brain or burning in your heart, congratulations. Your work is worthy.

Be sure to read about self-publishing options in Chapter 10.

Inspirational, Religious, and Metaphysical Books

Here's a genre that's wide open to good writers, but it's not for wimps. Unlike how-to and self-help genres, in which you can put a new twist on a tried-and-true concept and turn out a book, writing a specialty book in one of these categories requires that you be closely attuned to your readership. With inspirational, religious, and metaphysical books, you have to be especially clear about your audience, language, and marketing.

Research the market. Which publishers buy your type of book? Most large publishing houses, such as Simon and Schuster, have divisions, called *imprints*, for this genre. Some medium-sized and smaller houses do not handle the genre at all. If you were to send your inspirational proposal to a house that doesn't ever publish the genre, regardless of the brilliance of your work, you would have just wasted the cost of postage. That's why it is essential to go on that bookstore field trip. This is work, but you must find books that hold some similarity to yours to discover appropriate publishers for your book.

If you come up with publishers that have imprints for your genre or have published other books in the same vein, then you've struck pay dirt. Now you know to whom you will send your proposal. (If you're working with an agent, that person will most likely do a lot of this work for you, yet it's always smart to know this information yourself.) Once you find a publisher who seems like a good match for your project, you may want to call the sales office on their toll-free phone number and request a catalogue. Some publishers have websites with all the information as close as your keyboard. The catalogue or website will tell about the titles, prices, length, and authors of their books. You can also connect to an Internet bookstore, such as BarnesandNoble.com and Amazon.com, to research books, publishers, and genres.

Where have you seen books similar to yours? Were they only in a Christian or religious bookstore? In the new-age stores? On the shelf marked *Inspirational Books* at your bookstore? Smart writers attempt to write books that can be cross-marketed to more than one area.

Learn your topic well. Before you begin to write the proposal for your book, you must have a complete grasp of the terms, definitions, history, theory, and contemporary results of books in your genre. In this specialized area, don't just take one definition as the only one. Often, for instance, one religious or metaphysical group may have a far different take on a topic yet use the same term.

Within the genre are subgenres too. As an illustration, the inspirational book *365 Reflections on Marriage*, the book I collected and edited for Bob Adams Media, falls into the subgenre of a collection of quotes from notable women. Then there are self-help inspirational books like Mary Manin Morrissey's *Building Your Field of Dreams* (Bantam), and motivational books, with Julia Cameron's *The Artist's Way* (Tarcher/Putnam) heading the list.

If you understand the genre and can write books that touch the heart, you can do very well in this area that's growing by leaps and bounds.

True Crime Books

Writers of this genre live by this adage: Truth is stranger than fiction. Americans can't seem to get enough true crime books, and if you enjoy writing in a punchy, journalistic style, this is the genre for you.

As with the inspirational, religious, and metaphysical markets, you'll have to do research to make a sale. Most true crime books use plenty of fiction-style writing methods, but they do not distort what really happened. The crime is only one part of the book. The cast of characters, from the victim to the suspect, all have to be unforgettable to the reader. We want to know who, why, when, where, and how the crime was committed, and we don't want any sugar coating on the details.

If the victim was harassed by a grandmotherly stalker who was deranged because everyone trampled her zinnias, we want to see just how Grandma did it. We want to see her peeking into windows, hunkered down in the shrubs, and calling the victim's name over the back fence.

If the suspect wore green shorts, red suspenders, and a camera around her neck and always carried a golf club, let us know why she dressed this way. What was on the roll of film when it was developed? Were the suspenders the murder weapon? Why didn't she just use the golf club to knock the victim senseless?

When writing true crime books, you'll need to interview witnesses, and perhaps the victim and the suspect. If you're about to launch a book in this genre, be sure to check out the interview tips included in Chapter 8.

You'll also need to become a smart researcher, understand the lingo of the crime's type, and be able to explain the entire business of the crime in an intriguing, page-turning way. Be sure to read books by your fellow writers in this field to see the depth of their research.

Unlike other nonfiction genres, if you plan to write true crime, you may want to read some police procedural mysteries to get a feel for the pacing of a novel. Yes, you're writing about an actual event, but if you leave out the action, motivation, and resolutions, you won't sell your book.

Get Permission to Include That Photo

Let's say you're writing a true crime book, a celebrity book, or even a how-to book. It may be appropriate to include photos in your book. You'll need to get permission to include each photo from the people in the photos, even if you were the photographer. Some publishers want you to send photo releases along with the photos. (A similar form is used for permission to publish information and quotations resulting from an interview. A sample interview release form is presented in Chapter 8 — Successful Interviewing.)

Create or use a photo release. Here's what it should include:

PHOTO RELEASE

I, _____ *[photo subject's name inserted here]*, give my permission to _____ *[your name should go here]* to use my photograph in conjunction with the book, _____ *[your book's title or working title goes here]*. I understand that no payment is expected for the use of the photo. I do not wish to see the photo before the book is submitted to the editor.

_____   _____

Author   Date

It's not necessary to get the individual whose photo will appear in the book to preapprove the photos; often it's done as a courtesy, however. Keep a copy of the release on file after you submit the manuscript and additional material (such as interview releases) to your publisher. A photo release can also be a simple typed form stating the person's name and the fact that you have paid this individual so much for modeling, or that no money is expected for this service. Have the form signed and dated.

Celebrity Books

Athletes, film and television actors, politicians, medical professionals, and anyone who has experienced or done something significant are grouped into this genre. These are the books about the people we know from the screen or read about in *People* magazine or the newspaper.

The celebrity book might be a how-to, such as those in which *Wheel of Fortune*'s Vanna White endorses crochet patterns, or it might be a kiss-and-tell book (a style of biography) about the newest Hollywood heartbreaker.

The key to writing and selling celebrity books is to do the obvious: Be in contact with a celebrity who is well known enough to warrant a book. If you want to write celebrity books, figure out how you'll pitch your idea, and then contact the celebrity. Sure, that's not easy at times, but it can be done. The Screen Actor's Guild and the American Medical Association are two groups that keep lists of their members.

When you talk with celebrities or their representatives, be ready to defend your writing background and experience and what you can bring to the table. Let's say you want to write a travel book with someone like Bill Cosby. If you're currently the editor of a large travel magazine or have already written about travel — and celebrities — you'll probably get a nod of interest. If you've never written anything at all, never traveled outside of your county's boundaries, and don't know Mr. Cosby from the guy next door, you may as well forget it.

Prepare yourself well. Many notable people are hounded by the press and people like you and me, who watch their every move.

All that understood, if you have a smashing idea, go for it. I am the first to urge you to just jump in where the timid won't step. You could fail, yes, but you might be surprised at the way it works out.

A few years ago I came up with the idea of a book that dispensed the quirky wisdom and advice of *Golden Girls* and Broadway star Estelle Getty. I contacted her theatrical agent through the Screen Actor's Guild and shared my book idea. Miss Getty was even more wonderful in person than she seemed on television and the stage. She was a delight to be with. We spoke on the phone about the topic a few times, then met at her home and talked some more. We had a publisher nibbling on the book, and then Miss Getty was asked to appear in a weekly sitcom. Within days of this news, a book I'd proposed to a publisher months before was accepted. For both reasons, the book with Estelle Getty never materialized. Moral? Even great ideas and wonderful celebrities sometimes fail to make it into print.

 ## Increase Productivity

A tip that may not often be seen in a book on writing is this: Take care of yourself.

An hour of tennis or nine holes of golf, a zoo trip with the kids, a phone call to your spouse to share a bit of news, a chat with a friend during lunch time, all work wonders to keep your mind sharp and body refreshed.

Staying healthy, eating a smart diet, and exercising also give you the stamina you need to increase productivity. If you do no other form of exercise, take a walk every day. As you're walking, boost your ego with affirmations, think through a knotty writing problem, or mentally organize your workday. Give some thanks for the fact that you have opportunities and have another day to write.

Self-employed writers need vacations and weekends off, an afternoon at the beach, a trip to the shopping mall, and a bag of popcorn while sitting at the ball park. This downtime is necessary, just like recess was when we were in elementary school.

Travel Books

Travel experts forecast that air travel alone will increase 50 percent between 2000 and 2007. It may be that baby boomers will have more time in retirement and with the kids off on their own. Or perhaps we've made the world feel smaller with all the global connections at our fingertips via the Internet. Who knows? But it's great news for those who like to write in this genre. With more people traveling, more travel books will be in demand.

Within the travel book genre are: adventure books, how-to books, location guides, and travel/food/inspirational books. Each of these subsets has further divisions. As an example, location guides can be about a city, region, or national monument, but they can also be travel guides to parks, gardens, restaurants, and the best places to kiss.

If you're planning to write a book in the travel genre, you'll need to put a fresh spin on the topic and find a territory that hasn't been written to death. Look at your own passions and hobbies. Let's say you're a *Star Trek* fan, in a big way. You might want to write a book about attending the Trekkie conventions, portraying all the sights and sounds and people and creatures. You'll want to discuss how to dress for a convention (and advise your readers that they can do better than appear as Captain Kirk), and offer suggestions about what to buy, including the costly collectibles.

If you're an Elvis fan, you might write a travel book about Elvis sightings. He isn't really dead, you know — just ask his devotees. Or if you love to hike, cycle, swim, kayak, or climb mountains, and can write about these activities for others, you can share great information and advice about unique places to go.

Travel books don't just happen. Typically, those that are published today are not rambling, meandering tales of journeys, but instead they supply all the information and tips one needs to recreate the trip or visit the location. As with other genres, you'll need to research the market and understand the specific methods of writing travel books before you begin.

When I collaborated with another writer on *The Insiders' Guide to San Diego* (Falcon Press/Insiders'Guides), the book was to follow a formula made successful by other writers of books in the series. Initially, one writer, who was working on another regional book for Insiders' Guides, saw only the restrictions the formula seemed to impose on the creative endeavor. A few colleagues even asked if there was any margin for creativity. Yes, we were expected to follow certain chapter topics, but we had some latitude — we were able to pick and choose the material that was noteworthy about our hometown and our county. If we had written the book with only facts, figures, and information, it would have been as dry as burnt toast. Instead we quoted local experts, sought out annual events with diverse cultural and ethnic flavors, shared restaurants and resorts where we take only our favorite people. We described tidbits of stirring history. We revealed little-known areas of San Diego and proved that the area is more than just another pretty California city. We had fun.

When writing travel books, you must be able to write about more than the place or event. You have to concoct word pictures to bring the place and adventure right into your reader's mind. If you don't do this, the book won't work.

Author Frances Mayes paints word pictures in a way that transports us to her renovated villa in *Under the Tuscan Sun* (Broadway). We feel like we're helping her pick green olives and mix cement to repair a ruined wall; we can almost taste the red wine we're sipping as we bask in the warmth of the afternoon sun. In his book, *Into Thin Air* (Anchor), Jon Krakauer scares the willies out of those of us who are sensible enough *not* to climb Mt. Everest. Brrr, we're chilled by the experience without ever leaving the living room. Bill Bryson's *A Walk in the Woods* (Broadway) elicits chuckles from us as he becomes caught up in the environmental issues of the day. In Mike McIntyre's *The Kindness of Strangers* (Berkeley), about a journalist trekking across America, relying only on the kindness of strangers for food, shelter, and an occasional ride, we perceive the wheels of his journey, we perceive each obstacle. We marvel at the sometimes tilted logic of fellow humans.

All these travel books are about real people and real places, written in a way that the messages fly off the page and into our brains. Your job as a travel book writer is to translate the emotion of the journey into words. To do this you must use all the senses.

You must also be ready for the possibility of rejection. Some people will love to tell you that travel books don't sell. You have my permission to shout back that Bryson, Mayes, and McIntyre, among others, can make a living selling books about places and trips. Why, you might even tell them that I've written about my own hometown.

 ## Specialty Language

Each genre and subgenre has its own *language*. Its fruitless and frustrating to submit a book proposal directed to a specific market if you don't know the special words or buzz words — or what they mean.

Before you undertake a book that includes specialty language, begin your own *book word list*: Write down and then define the words for your specific field. You can learn more about the right and wrong use of buzz words from dictionaries, trade publications, and your competitor's books. If the words you're using have unusual definitions, you may want to forward the list to your editor when you submit your manuscript so that you both will be clear on the meanings.

Cooking and Food Books

Some readers pour over cookbooks, collecting, reading about, and relishing the imagined tastes of the foods described on each page. The cookbook and food book market is huge, and if you can make what we eat sound even better than the actual dish, you have what it takes to write for this genre. To succeed, according to those who specialize in cookbooks, you have to produce "drool" copy.

Writing as a Second Career

Are you retired, a computer whiz, a disabled teenager, a parent, or a therapist? If you're any of these things, to name a few, you are an expert. Use your expertise to write as a second career.

A writer who spent twenty years as a bookkeeper is writing a book on bookkeeping methods for the small business owner. A fire marshal is also the publisher of books for the fire protection industry. A school teacher writes and sells humor and gift books.

Turn your hobbies and your passions into books. Use your interests as a leaping-off point to investigate the nonfiction book field. Remember, it's lovely if you're already an expert, but it's not essential. A healthy quest for information, a dusting of creative know-how, and good writing habits make writers successful.

As always, in-person and Internet field trips to bookstores are in order if you want to write a cookbook or food book. It's essential to know what's out there and understand the trends. If you were to produce yet another book on cooking using less fat and oil, the competition with the other "lite" cookbooks would be stiff. Give your book a twist, perhaps collaborating with a formerly overweight celebrity who now uses only olive oil with which to cook, and you might have the slant to sell a book.

Reread the earlier section in this chapter on inspirational, religious, and metaphysical books. You'll need to follow the same advice for researching and understanding the competition, locating specific publishers, and putting a curve on your book to make it marketable.

As we discussed in Chapter 2, I anticipate that the current trend of cookbooks that tell family stories, share ethnic recipes, and give self-help information along with recipes will continue to the next decade and beyond. If you have the family Bible that has Grandfather's recipe for plum pudding or grilled guppy, which he concocted while crossing the dust bowl in the thirties, you may have the material right at hand for a best-selling food book.

You'll want to spend time outlining and brainstorming ways to write your book. Suggestions for giving your book a marketable edge are found in Chapter 6. Good luck and bon appetit.

Describe That Person

When writing nonfiction we often have to write about the people who people our work. To increase the strength of your "characterization" muscles, do this exercise about someone you're currently writing about. If you're not writing about an individual, do the exercise for someone you know or would like to know, or would like to have known, from Albert Einstein to Clara Bow.

Step 1. Fill in blanks for each of the items below. You'll want to do this exercise more than once, so make plenty of photocopies of this page (especially if you've borrowed this book from a friend).

Step 2. After you have completed each item below and discovered the inner being of your chosen person, write a page about this individual. For extra credit: Focus your writing on the person's most quirky characteristic.

Person's name: _____

Most identifying feature: _____

_____

Most remarkable characteristic: _____

_____

This person is from: _____

When I think of this person, I always remember the time: _____

_____

Favorite color: _____

The look of his or her eyes can tell: _____

_____

This person's most gratifying moment was when: _____

_____

The biggest challenges in this person's life have been: _____

_____

When asked about the past, this person might say: _____

_____

When asked about the future, this person would say: _____

_____

Favorite food: _____

To describe the way this person dresses, I have to be able to say: _____

_____

A thumbnail sketch of this person's physical appearance is: _____

_____

A sketch of this person's emotional and spiritual state is: _____

_____

This person's favorite author, movie star, politician: _____

_____

Spare time is spent doing: _____

Favorite spot on the planet: _____

This person would like to be remembered for: _____

_____

CHAPTER 6

Who Is Your Reader?

When you cease to make a contribution
you begin to die.
— Eleanor Roosevelt

When you are writing, who counts more: you or your reader? The answer is, you both count. Every book project requires a commitment to complete it, do the best work possible, and connect well with the public. Readers have a say-so in your relationship too. When they pick up your book, they are asking you to come into their lives. They give you their trust. They give you permission to share information.

Every experience we have changes us in some way. As you read through this book, it is my hope that you may have a few revelations about what it takes to write nonfiction books or rediscover some useful writing techniques. The writer's goal is to enter the reader's head. Depending on the way the book is written, the effect lingers or it doesn't. You get your point across or you don't. Normally, the "don'ts" never get their books published, because editors are shrewd about readers' needs and desires.

Editors are smart about targeting readers because that's the only way editors can make a living, yet many writers forget this fact. They get so involved in their work that they neglect to write for the reader. Big mistake.

In this chapter we are going to talk about who your reader is: how to identify your reader and how to use this information to increase the chances that your book will sell. We'll also discuss how to focus on specific points you want to cover in your book and how to brainstorm for fresh ideas. Finally, we'll pass on some tips for marketing your book that need to be built into the text as you write.

Targeting and Identifying Your Audience

Who is your reader? That's a question I always ask every one of my writing students. Actually, I make a really big deal out of it, and some students think I belabor the point. But if you can't imagine *clearly* who will buy your book, you have a problem — and perhaps not enough material or the best slant for a book. You're going to have to write about your targeted reader for the book proposal. Take time to make notes about this person right now, and you'll avoid anguish later.

You also need to be sure that more than a small segment of the population will want to buy your book. For discussion only, let's say you're writing a how-to book on tuning a tuba. The tuba is a marvelous instrument and its history is rich with the musical flavor of Wagner and Sousa. How many people, however, are going to buy a book on tuning a tuba? How many tuba tuners are there in the United States? Although not all books are published to make money for the publisher and the writer, normally that is the objective. A book must be broad enough in context to bring in readers, and enough books must be sold to make the project financially worthwhile.

If you're considering writing a book that will have a limited readership, you may want to broaden the scope or re-think the project to make it marketable. For example, our tuba-tuning book could be expanded to a broader readership: We could write it to encompass how to adjust, maintain, repair, and restore all brass and brass-wind instruments. Thus we have targeted a much larger readership and increased the chances of cross-marketing. *Cross-marketing* simply means writing your book for more than one market. Book buyers might range from the musical instrument tuner to the repair person to the hobbyist who restores brass instruments. Of course, broadening the scope of the project is more work for the writer, but with a wider readership identified, the book will become more appealing to a publisher.

Once you understand the readers who will buy your book, narrow your focus.

- Who is the real reader? Depending on your topic it might be a sports fan, a physician, a parent, a stamp collector. When you identify the exact person, look closer.

- What are the reader's book-buying habits?

- What does the reader like or dislike in a book?

- What do you need to know about this reader, the consumer of your product, to make the book more enticing?

You've been on that field trip we talked about in Chapter 2. You've seen all the books in the store, and most large stores have more than 20,000 books on hand. Those books are your competition for a reader's dollars. It pays to know how best to write the book for that person.

To find out how to write a book for your reader, you'll have to do some research, unless you're sure you already know what the reader will buy. With luck you can access one of the Internet bookstores, like Amazon.com, and search for titles that belong to your future competitors. Some Internet bookstores provide lists of similar titles that previous buyers have also purchased.

Your next step is to try to figure out why people are buying those books. For example, if the bookstore's customer bought XYZ book and ABC book, how are the books similar, beyond their parallel topics? Are they written by the same author? Do

they have clear how-to instructions? Do they give a different
view, or more views, of the topic?

You can also find information about your consumer's
reading preferences by researching *Reader's Guide to Periodic
Literature.* Now online at most public libraries, this book lists
articles from many popular magazines by topic, title, and
author. Once you discover that your future reader bought a
specific book, take this information to *Reader's Guide* and find
out if the author of that book has published any articles on the
same topic, a method followed by smart authors. (See Chapter
12 for tips on this essential step in the book-writing business.)
Go ahead and read the articles.

Study the advertisements in the magazine. From the
advertisements you gain more insight about the reader. If the
article was published in *Sports Illustrated*, you'll get a picture
of the reader. If it appears in a church periodical, you can
visualize the potential reader. Likewise, if the article shows up
in a magazine that sells shady advertisements and prints
articles of a dubious nature, you'll be able to form a portrait of
your reader, perhaps in a new, unfavorable way. Looking at
the advertisements and the editorial content of magazines can
open a new world in which to identify your future readership.

When I write, I keep a clear picture of my reader in my mind
with every sentence. I can see you sitting there, on the
commuter bus bouncing along or at your desk during lunch
break, the book's pages dog-eared at the important places. Or
you might be sitting in the living room, nestled in an
overstuffed chair, trying to ignore the music blaring from your
teenager's bedroom.

I understand you have already been given both good and
inferior advice on writing books. I sense your feelings of
trepidation. I appreciate you, too, when I visualize you
scratching your head over a point I haven't made clear. I can
hear you say, "Would you explain that?" It's kind of spooky,
isn't it? I know you. When you write your book you need to
get that close to your reader, too.

Now that you're getting to know your reader, your goal is to write in a way the reader enjoys. That could mean using complex sentences and theories, colorful language, illustrations and anecdotes, or other techniques appropriate to your specific genre. Books don't come with ratings as do movies, so you will need to make it clear to the publisher, in your proposal, and in the book, whether you're out to capture the G audience, the X-rated one, or readers somewhere in between.

Writers who fail to place books with the best publisher usually do so because they have forgotten the reader. Be smart. Do not neglect this important part of your research.

Who *Is* That Person?

As you focus on your reader, make notes about this person, from gender to educational level, from career to hobby choice. When you begin to write, keep in mind that food analogies work especially well with many women readers, most guys respond well to sports images, often teens understand comparisons to music and movies, and kids will get your point when you talk about toys.

If your book about assisted-living options for aging parents is geared to 30 to 40 year olds, and you compare the inhumane conditions of some unlicensed housing to the 1948 black and white movie *The Snake Pit* (about atrocious mental institutions of the past), you'll leave your reader in the dark. Compare the housing to the feeling of being crammed into a New York subway train at rush hour, and your image will be clear.

Determining the Topics and Points of Your Book

If the publishing world were perfect — and it's not, in case you're wondering — what would you like to include in your book? That is the next step in getting ready to write.

- Have you listed everything you want to include and hope to achieve?

- What points will you cover?

- Want do you want to stress? Avoid?

- What is your focus?

When writing *Eve of Destruction: Prophecies, Theories, and Preparations for the End of the World* (Lowell House), I wrote as a historian and a journalist. I reviewed concepts and explained the past. Further, I chose a writing style that would be comfortable for my reader, who was the same person who buys *TV Guide* and *USA Today*. These folks want the human story behind the story, and that's what I gave them. I didn't put in my two cents because that wasn't the direction I wanted to take. My goal was to present information in a way readers could understand and then come to their own conclusions.

Throughout the writing process, go back and refocus on your objectives and how you're fulfilling them. It's not unusual to lose sight of your target — that is where a thesis statement and outline keep you on track.

Sit down right now and write the major concepts of your book, in broad brush strokes. On this same paper, describe what your reader wants in the book. Be honest. The two might not mesh. Once you have these ideas down, your formatting has begun. Now go directly to the next section on brainstorming.

Brainstorming

The bubble method, clustering, and mind mapping are all the same thing — powerful, creative tools smart writers of both nonfiction and fiction use to discover the unexpected and to clarify thoughts.

The bubble method works whether you are brainstorming for a book, a book's chapter, interview questions to ask experts, or book titles. If there is one part of this book I'll keep my fingers crossed that you'll use, it's this one. People in my writing classes gush about the concept, and yet it's deceptively simple.

Creative Bubbling

Here are the directions to brainstorm for a book. If you're brainstorming for a chapter, book titles, or another creative endeavor, just substitute the focus.

1. Get a large piece of plain newsprint paper and crayons or colored markers. You may not use typing paper and pens. You need to *think big*.
2. Print the topic of your book in the middle of the piece of paper. Draw a circle around the words. Add ten lines straight out from the circle, or the first bubble. You have made what looks like a child's drawing of the sun with a word in the center.
3. Without censoring yourself in any way, write ten subtopics that are somehow related to your main topic. Do not stop with seven or nine. You must brainstorm until you have ten topics out there. Circle them, too. That's it. Simple and powerful.
4. Sit back and look at the fresh ideas the system produced.

   Let's say you started out wanting to write a book on home brewing, so you put the words *home brew* in the middle bubble. Off the words came an assortment of topics from pilsner to ale to history to contests. Then, out of nowhere, popped *hygiene*, a topic essential to pure, drinkable beer. Had you not bubbled, you might have forgotten to address this issue, which might have meant that your intended publisher would think you didn't know the basics.
5. After you have looked over your second set of bubbles, select those that seem to be meaty enough to support an entire chapter. You'll probably come up with seven to ten. If you cannot comfortably include

seven, return to step one or consider doing more research to learn about your proposed topic.

6. Take each of the sub-bubbles individually and bubble again. With this go-round you're actually outlining your chapters, and you'll come up with seven to ten main topics for each chapter.

7. If necessary, so that you're comfortable beginning the writing process from this outline method, bubble down further and outline your sub-sub-bubbles.

8. After you've bubbled and feel comfortable with the focus of the book, put the entire thing away for a day or so, if you can. Try not to consciously think about the bubbles during this time. I promise your brain will be silently churning out massive loads of creativity.

9. Without looking at the previous bubbles, go back and repeat the entire process.

10. Finally, compare the two. Then put the material in a list form on your computer, and you'll have a map or outline that will successfully take you to the completion of your book.

Try the bubble method for unique titles and titles of the chapters, too. The system is easy and fun and quick and addictive.

Outline Methods

Although the bubble method is my thumbs-up creative choice, sometimes I do go back to the old-fashioned method we all used in high school. Outlining isn't creative and it doesn't require much imagination, but sometimes you have a topic that just requires it. For example, books that are sequential, such as history or educational books, almost demand outlining because one part or event must be built on the previous one. If the 1, 2, 3, a, b, c method does the job for you, go for it.

You can also sit at your computer and list, in no particular order, every conceivable topic under the sun that you might want to include in your book. Then you can go back and put the topics into some order. Or, if you have an exceptionally organized brain, you may be able to keep the whole book roughly in your head. If so, then use this method.

Some writers write outline notes on three- by five-inch cards and then organize the cards into the correct sequence. Some make folders, identify the folders with a chapter title or number, and then, as the book's research develops, slip notes into the folders.

With the word-processing program I use, I can have the manuscript in one window or screen, and the outline in another window so that I can refer to it as I write. I consult the outline often. I might also print out the outline so I can quickly glance down at it from time to time, scratch off each subtopic as I write, or make notes on the sheet. I like to copy and paste the topics from my outline to the beginning of each chapter. When I have finished one subtopic and hit the *Enter* key, I can instantly see what is next.

Whatever outlining method you choose, if you find that it works, continue to use it, because your outline keeps you on track. The outline is your map.

Few people would gas up the car in Chicago and head south for a vacation in New Orleans without packing a map. I have been on some of those highways and it's still easy to get sidetracked. When I write, I take detours and modify as I move through the manuscript, just as you or I might stop to visit a national park or tourist attraction along the route. But I also know that unless I follow that outline — my map — my trip won't turn out as I planned.

Writing and Money and Success

Don't let anyone's preconceived opinion of literary integrity and the artistry of writing keep you from making a living in this field. Initially you may not get a huge advance and be able to quit your day job; few of us have had that luxury. But you can achieve your own level of success.

A pitfall for many writers and other artistic people is to measure success in dollar signs. They do not equate. Get that straight right now and you will be better off. And don't think because you have to hold down two jobs — writing and the *other job* — that you're not a successful writer. Few nonfiction and fiction writers, unless they live simply, have learned to turn out enough work to enjoy a satisfying, comfortable lifestyle. For some, that's a cabin in New Mexico without running water or indoor toilets. Yes, I know a writer who chooses to live like this, and she's a wonderful, sane person too.

For me, a successful life means being able to plan for the future, have money for my needs and pleasures and an occasional vacation, and write as a career. I get to work at home, visit with friends and family when I want, travel to exotic and interesting places, swap intelligent and crazy ideas with intelligent and crazy people, play with my dogs, volunteer, make baby afghans for a relief program, support various nonprofit groups, and tend my roses. To add to my income, I also consult with private writing clients, take on individual students who are serious about their writing craft, and teach at the university, seminars, and conferences. Ben Franklin said, "If you want something done, give it to a busy person." I'm busy and I get stuff done.

Learn to budget your time and your money. Take to heart the time- and money-saving tips sprinkled through this book. Write every day, even on those days when you're not in the mood, and you will succeed. I promise you. You will.

Selecting a Title

Book titles cannot be copyrighted. If you wanted to give your newest book the same title as this book, you could legally do so. Yet, it's not smart to even consider it. You want your book to be special and have a title that reflects your topic.

I call the process of deciding on the title for a book, *naming the baby.* Your baby's name — your book title — needs to speak to the reader, describe your topic, and be fresh. Selecting a title that captures the literary agent's eye or publisher's interest is your goal. A dreary or dismal title won't stop a sale, but a great title can add sizzle and quite possibly make the sale.

Titles are normally five words or less; some have subtitles. When you're considering a title, visualize it on the spine of the book. On a bookstore shelf where only the spine will show, would you be able to tell what your book is about from those words alone?

Tips for Terrific Titles

1. Titles are labels, headlines, and calling cards.
2. Too often, readers, editors, and agents only read titles before selecting what to read.
3. Key phrases, lists (that is, Ten Ways to . . .), snappy word twists, provocative questions can become great titles.
4. Sometimes the title just won't "happen," but once the book is complete, it appears.
5. Come up with several titles. Print them out. Tack them on the bulletin board so you can see how they look. And say them out loud. If your tongue can't make it through a title, an editor's won't either.

Editors are notorious for changing book titles. Unless this is your tenth book or you have a strong publishing record, you may not have the luxury of getting the title you choose. Remember, publishers are in the business of designing and naming books to make them irresistible to the buying public.

Some writers become title collectors, working at titles to sharpen them. Some don't even have book topics in mind when they begin brainstorming or collecting titles. These people keep title lists in their writer's journals or in files on their computers.

Here's a list of title categories:

How-to titles	Rhyming titles	Frightening titles
Shock titles	Trick titles	Silly titles
Question titles	Short titles	Punch-line titles
List titles	Item titles	Statistic titles

Be sure to run your perfect title idea through *Books in Print* to make sure there aren't already a dozen of them out there. But if you absolutely love your title, and you find a duplicate in *Books in Print*, go ahead and use it anyway. When I selected the title *For the Love of Children* (Health Communications), I discovered there were two other books that had that title too. But it was perfect, and the publisher and I decided to keep it, nonetheless.

Write Your Own Review

It doesn't matter how far along you are with your nonfiction book, whether you're starting with a nugget of an idea or have a finished manuscript, try this creative exercise.

Pretend you are the book reviewer from the newspaper or Writer's Digest magazine. Write a review of your book. There is only one rule: You must praise the book, the topic, the writing, and the author. This is a positive book review.

If you can't remember the style in which books are reviewed, check out magazines such as Bloomsbury Review, Publisher's Weekly, and Library Journal.

Make your review at least 500 words long. Do not show it to anyone. As you write your nonfiction book, reflect on it and your success.

CHAPTER 7

Organizing Your Book

If you would not be forgotten
as soon as you are dead,
either write things worth reading or
do things worth writing.
— Benjamin Franklin

Brainstorming, as we talked about in the last chapter, is one of the most creative ways to develop your book from a spark of energy to an idea to a manuscript. Even with your first attempt at the bubble method, you'll come up with ideas that feel fresh and workable.

The outlines and brainstorming techniques discussed in the last chapter will get you started and help you organize your creative concepts. But to produce a book you have to have a plan. That's what this chapter is all about — the nuts and bolts of physically transforming your creative juices into chapters, sidebars, and expert advice, along with editing practices and working with a manageable timeline. Do you want to finish the book you're creating? This chapter tells you how.

Reviewing Chapter Styles

We've talked about the style of writing and book formats, now let's get down to the nitty-gritty of chapters. When reviewing other books in your genre, you noticed there are significant differences in form and function, that is, in the way the text is presented. In this book, you've seen how the material is divided into chapters for each general topic, and then there are subtopics, such as the heading, *Reviewing Chapter Styles*, above. Sometimes books have chapters, sometimes they have sections, and sometimes they have divisions like programs or parts.

As you think about the division of your book, keep in mind that chapters should be approximately the same length. That means if Chapter One of your manuscript is 5,000 words long or 20 typed pages, all other chapters should be about the same length. This is the style American readers are most comfortable with and what publishers expect you to do.

 ## Chapters Should Match

Chapters should be approximately the same length, but how does one do that? Actually, it's a snap.

Let's say your book is going to be approximately 70,000 words — the most popular length for contemporary nonfiction. You have ten chapters. Divide 70,000 by ten and you'll see that every chapter needs to be about 7,000 words. Further, if you have seven subtopics per chapter, divide 7,000 words per chapter by seven, and you'll know that every subtopic must be approximately 1,000 words, about the size of a short magazine article. Even for those of us who are mathematically challenged, this system works.

No, all chapters will not be exactly a certain number of words, but you'll want to come close because that's the current style for nonfiction books. And if you ever feel overwhelmed about the amount of material needed for your book, think of it in pieces, like small magazine articles grouped together.

As you consider how you want your book to be written, you also need to decide on style. We're not talking design issues, such as fonts and page layout, or the style of language. Rather, you need to select the subject matter of each chapter and how the information will be presented.

The best way to do that is to review books you enjoy and find out what there is about the text that's positive and appealing. Do you like numbered lists, bullets, and boxed information that lead the eyes to important data? While the pretty icons and thickness of the box frames are design issues, writers must build the boxes and bulleted lists into the manuscript. Do you like quotes at the beginning of each chapter? Do summaries at the end of the chapters make the genre in which you're writing more accessible? Are there places for the reader to write or to take notes, which make your concept interactive? What makes the text appealing?

An example of what works can easily be seen in cookbooks. Traditionally, before a recipe is presented, there is a bit about it, perhaps a narrative about the origins of the recipe or some mouth-watering prose about the tastes of the dish. After that the actual ingredients are stated, followed by how the recipe should be prepared. A cookbook buyer expects the information to be presented in a sequential and easy-to-follow manner. Naturally there are recipe books that don't follow that formula, but most that sell do. Remember, you aren't stealing ideas when you look at successful books and decide that you want a similar look to your own book. You are stealing only if you take someone else's words, photos, or illustrations, and call them your own.

Learn from published authors what works for your genre.

Sidebars and Other Formats

A popular format option for the nonfiction book is to use the sidebar or information box. Like the ones you've seen in magazine articles, these give additional information that's easy to find and quick to read. Sidebars and boxes are popular in motivational books, computer books, travel books, and the always bestselling how-to book. I like them and so do readers. If you like the technique and your topic fits it, write them into your manuscript.

With your book still in the planning stage, consider what material might be used as sidebars or in boxes. Quotes? Questions? Case studies? How-to tips? Review other recently published books in your genre to see if and how sidebars or boxes are used and the type of material that is included. Some books use both techniques.

One of my favorite uses of sidebars and boxes in books is to give unexpected details that enhance the reader's experience. When writing

> ## A Sidebar Can Help You Highlight Information
>
> Your goal should be to include information that seems pertinent and noteworthy. Sometimes writers use sidebars and boxes for quotes — voices of people with ideas that support the topics in each chapter. You'll also see checklists, handy tips, time saving advice, toll-free information numbers, and the names and addresses of self-help or business groups.

on grief management in *What to Do When a Loved One Dies* (Dickens Press), I shared essays and short excerpts from other books to spark and challenge the reader's ideas on death. The reader could have checked the bibliography and found this information, but featured within the text of the book in sidebars, the material produced an instant "aha." I varied the information by adding a smattering of poetry.

When you work on the manuscript, don't use desktop publishing software to actually create a sidebar or box. Instead, in the text of your manuscript, indicate the approximate placement of the material. You do this by inserting a note to the editor suggesting that certain information be included in a sidebar in a specific spot. This note, in brackets, will look something like this: [Ed: Sidebar begins]. When you finish typing the information that should be included in the sidebar, in standard type and double-spaced like the rest of your manuscript, add the note: [Sidebar ends].

The final physical placement of the material will be determined when the publishing house's graphic designer establishes the layout of the book. Yet you know your topic best, and by indicating where you think a box or sidebar should go, you will help the editorial staff produce a better book.

As you ponder the style of your chapters, you'll discover whether the boxed information or sidebar concept works.

Illustrations and Photos

Are you going to use illustrations and/or photos in your book? Before you say yes, remember that they increase the publisher's production budget significantly. If you're self-publishing your book, you'll have to come to terms with that decision too.

To illustrate this point, let's say your book just has to have photos and illustrations. Many publishers do not pay extra for the services of photographers or illustrators; they believe the cost of using these professionals should come out of the writer's advance. Before you hire anyone, make sure you know who will be paying. While negotiating your publishing contract, you may be able to build in a photo or illustration budget and have your publisher pick up the bill.

You can hire a photographer or illustrator. These folks are working professionals with the same needs as writers, that is, to be paid promptly and fairly. Be prepared to outline exactly what you want, write up a contract, help coordinate the artistic endeavor, and pay fair wages. Some photographers and illustrators will allow you to use their work once, but they'll keep the copyright. Some will work for hire, and you'll be able to own the art. Make sure you know what you're buying so you can avoid mishaps.

To find reputable photographers and illustrators, contact professional organizations and talk with your publisher. The publisher may be able to recommend people who have worked on similar projects. If money is an issue, contact universities and colleges for photography or art students who may need to make some extra money. Again, you'll need to pay fair wages, and it's a good idea to get a few price quotes.

You can also access artwork and photos known as *clip art*, which can usually be used for no charge. Be sure to find out if there are any restrictions before using the clip art. In some cases you must get written permission and pay a fee if you use more than a few pieces. You can find clip art in books at the library and bookstore, and you can find some by browsing through various websites. Check your word-processing program too; most have at least some clip art.

Covering the Issue of Hardbound and Softbound

Being the author of a hardbound book may make you and your family proud, but today the book-buying public prefers softbound volumes. It's a matter of money.

If you're like most Americans and you have a choice between two good books — one hardbound, selling for $30 and up, or one softbound, selling for $10 to $15 — there's no contest. (The softbound book, which is usually larger, of better quality, and more expensive than a mass market paperback, is also referred to as a *trade paperback* or a *quality paperback.*)

Although some writers may imagine that producing hardbound books increases their prestige, it's really better to have softbound books to your credit. You'll make more royalties because people see softbound books as bargains and buy them more freely.

When sending a publisher illustrations or photos along with your manuscript, make it as easy as possible for the book designer to put the right artwork in the right place. You can do this with an *illustration guide*, a numbered list describing the illustrations.

In the illustration guide, each item is assigned a number and a name (if appropriate), and each illustration or photo should be marked with a number and name for cross-referencing. Of course, you don't want to mark directly on the illustration or photo; make the identification with easy-to-remove tape or a note on the back. Then in your text, include a placement cue for your editor or other staff person, which looks something like this: [Ed: Illustration #15, House and Child, goes here.]

If possible, keep duplicates of all camera-ready photos and illustrations that you send to the publisher, and definitely keep a copy of the list so you can identify the placement should the art get out of sequence. It's up to you, the writer, to organize these details.

Calculating the Book's Size

How is the length of a book determined? That's a question new nonfiction writers frequently ask. And rightly they should because the length of a book is nearly as important as the topic and your credentials. The length of a book is calculated by the concept, the competition, and the publisher's needs.

Paper, illustrations, photos, printing cost, shipping, and bookstore space all determine the size of the book the publisher wants to produce. If your vision of a book has illustrations and colored photos, be aware that the budget for that book will be considerably larger than the budget for a book with text only.

How much you know, want to share, and can write about a topic can decide the book's length. If you're working on *12,000 Blessings in Life*, a motivational book filled with affirmations, and have your heart set on seeing each blessing printed on its own page, you'll end up with 6,000-plus pages (because books are printed on both sides of the paper). That's a fat book, and most likely publishers will have other ideas.

The most successfully marketed books fall into a general range of length and size. It's important to know this when you're pitching your book in the proposal. Books that run approximately 60,000 to 80,000 words — about the length of this book, *Writing the Nonfiction Book*— are in the most demand by publishers because the public expects to pay a certain price for this size. These books sell for between $10 and $20, and are softbound.

This size book fits best on bookstore shelves. Oversized books, such as art and craft books, are more expensive to produce and may need more shelf space. As you already know, there's competition for space in bookstores so you want to make it easy to stock your book.

The length of the book is also determined by past books in the same genre. If all biographies are 100,000 words, and you propose one half that size, the publisher may be skeptical of your research. The buying public may not think they are getting their money's worth in a skinny book either. Of course, there are exceptions to this general rule, but keep the competitor's product in mind as you determine the length of your book.

The publisher may also dictate the length of your book if it's to be part of a series or genre marketing program. When I wrote *Resumes for Women*, the usual length of Arco/Prentice Hall's resume books was the determining factor. It had to fit into the series. If I had made it longer or shorter, it would have had to be a different price from Arco's other resume books. A lower price would mean less profit, as could a higher price, because the consumer might buy a competitive publisher's book over mine.

When you browse through the bookstore, look at the travel section for the *Insider's Guides* (Falcon Press). Note that each book, regardless of destination, is about the same thickness, so they all seem to be about the same length. Most are about 100,000 words, but some are longer. The width of the longer books was manipulated by the page layout, font size, and even the paper thickness.

Most book marketing specialists say books that are from 60,000 to 80,000 words long are the easiest to sell. When you're considering how to handle the subject matter, give length lots of thought. As you enter the field of nonfiction book writing, you will have the best chance of selling your book if you follow these practices. However, if you're going to write a longer book or a shorter one, and I've done both, address the length issue in your proposal.

Going Back to School for Writing

Should you take a creative writing class at a college? Most community colleges and universities offer creative writing classes. Many community colleges and parks and recreation departments offer writing programs, especially for senior citizens, at a low fee or even without cost. Most courses are extremely valuable for building confidence and providing the writer with a safe environment to write, read, and develop talent.

However, if you do attend creative writing classes, be conscious of when you've had enough — whether that's one semester or six. Don't allow the courses to become an excuse for never progressing or selling your work.

As an adult learner, you'll advance quicker than regular college students because you have an immediate need for the information. Use it and write. Writing is the best teacher.

Working Like a Writer

Do you fancy the idea of not having a boss hanging around while you work? Is creating your own flexible schedule appealing to you? If you've answered yes, you're in good company. Most writers and creative folks agree.

I am smitten with being my own boss. That was brought home to me just the other day when I was running Saturday errands on Tuesday. The stores were less busy. I got in and out of the cleaners without a wait. And the line at the post office was only a half mile long, rather than farther than the eye could see.

If you're like most writers, it feels great to be in charge of your career and your destiny. You have the luxury and the responsibility of working as hard or as easy as you choose, depending on the book project and the day. Managing a zillion pulls on your time becomes your responsibility. Important things, from getting your taxes ready for the IRS, to less important ones, like daytime TV shows, the garden, lunch with a loved one, bird watching, reading that steamy novel started the night before, and shopping, all can and will weasel into your writing time.

Failing or succeeding with your book project is also your responsibility. All your hopes and dreams can feel overwhelming. You might spend some sleepless nights wondering if your talents are strong enough, if you write well enough, and if have enough tenacity to stay put in that chair, facing your computer. It is worse, however, to give up and never experience the joy of writing, that humbling feeling when words and ideas appear in your work that scare or excite you, and you can't figure out where they came from.

What is a typical work day for a working writer? If you believe that most professionals do their best writing while sitting by a pool at their Beverly Hills mansion sipping drinks with tiny umbrellas sticking out of the glasses while being waited on by dazzling, brown-eyed pool attendants, think again. And if you think working writers get the most done as they snuggle near a crackling fire at a luxury lodge in Aspen, you've been watching too much television.

Most working writers spend more hours than we'll admit in front of our friend and nemesis, the computer. Most of us work without breaks, sometimes even on weekends and evenings. Most of us do not want to figure out how much we make as an hourly wage for fear that we would do better working at a fast-food joint. Remember that's why writing is called *work*. If it weren't hard to do, they would call it *play*. Nevertheless, most working writers cannot imagine working at any other profession.

Years ago as I researched a book, I met an entrepreneur who was then in her energetic eighties. Kathleen had more vigor and zest for life than most 20 year olds I've met. She was a captivating person, lovely inside and out.

Unaware of this lady's schedule at our first meeting, I naively asked, "Do you work part time?" She had a belly laugh at that one, replying, "Yes, I only work half a day; it doesn't matter which 12 hours I put in."

As a writer, you should relish this story because you're going to need to defend the fact that you do have a real job, even though you work part time. As a business owner, because that's what professional writers really are, you set your own hours and your own pace. You'll also be at the computer, library, or thinking while other family members, friends, and colleagues (of the non-writing ilk) are watching the big game, shopping, and vacationing.

Most of us get so caught up in the job of writing that we forget to:

- start dinner until the family tumbles through the door, hinting mutiny unless food appears fast.

- put on socks and shoes even when our feet are freezing.

- blink (people who spend time working on computers neglect to do so, then wonder why they get headaches).

- eat normal food at normal times.

People who work at non-creative jobs can't understand what goes on in a writer's brain, and they're often suspicious of it too. Inventiveness can be dangerous, at least so I'm told. Then again, we don't follow a traditional pattern of climbing that career ladder. We also enjoy, okay, let's be honest, hunger for, constantly covet, and lust after being alone. "Normal" people wonder about us for that. We love being able to work from our home offices.

When you attempt to explain how hard you work, you'll be scoffed at by those who believe that anyone with a #2 pencil and a legal pad can become the next bestselling nonfiction writer. Like Kathleen and me, you'll often work half days, getting those 12 hours in however you can.

Treat yourself like a professional who is writing a book, and do so even if you only have time to write one page a day. Subscribe to and read magazines for writers. Take classes on specific areas of writing, from how to produce dazzling dialogue to the intricacies of book promotion. Then take a bigger step and buy books on your craft and read about creativity. You'll find a handy list of recommended reading at the back of this book.

Make plans now to attend book signings and writing workshops — we can all learn new tricks of this trade. Go to writing conferences where you'll meet and mingle with top-notch writers, editors, and publishers. In every May issue and posted on their website (www.writersdigest.com), *Writer's Digest* publishes a list of conferences for writers. If you're reading this in December, go directly to your library and borrow or browse through the back issue for information, and make a photocopy of the listing to take home and study. Then call the staffers at the conferences that tickle your interest and get a brochure. Talk with other writers in your circle. Maybe you can go as a group or share accommodations.

Forget the mindset that if you talk about how you write, you may give away secrets. The only secret to writing is actually hitting the keyboard and producing a marketable product. Swap positive, helpful information with colleagues and others in the publishing profession.

Don't let yourself get dragged down by the negative attitudes of others — you do have a choice. When I attended a writing symposium a few years back, I spoke with some fiction writers. Because I put most of my creative energy into the nonfiction arena, I was interested in hearing what *the other side* had to say. These three griped about editors, publishers, and publicists, and how poor writers never get an even break. Sure, it's fun to swap war stories with those who are in the trenches, and we all do it, but this conversation wasn't productive. I already know what's wrong with the publishing industry (for one thing, its accounting methods are slower than molasses in January).

However, I choose to make my living in the field — no one is forcing me to be a writer. If it becomes uncomfortable to do so or it makes me unhappy, I'll get the heck out of Dodge and get into another profession. I refuse to bellyache about what's wrong with my career choice because I control my future. Just as you do.

The moral of this saga: You're going to meet people who love to dish out dirt about writing and publishing. You'll have to make a decision as to where you stand.

Read About Writers

If you would like an insider's scoop on how writers work, I highly recommend *Booknotes: America's Finest Authors on Reading, Writing, and the Power of Ideas*, edited by Brian Lamb, host of C-SPAN's *Booknotes*, and published by Random House, 1997. Be sure to watch the television show too. You'll see that the feelings you have about the craft of writing are also alive and thriving in others.

Making and Achieving Deadlines

You are your own boss, so it's up to you to set guidelines, prioritize your work load, and produce a book on time. You've signed a publishing contract and promised to have the book to the editor on a specific day. If you fail to do so, you could invalidate your contract. You might even have to return your advance.

Even before you get a publishing contract, set up a schedule
for writing. Before you write a word of your book, figure out
where, when, and how long each day you will write.
Remember, if you produce just one page a day for a year,
you'll have a book that's 365 pages long. Now think about
producing four pages a day for six months, and you'll get the
picture of what you could produce.

As you deveop a writing schedule, be honest. You cannot
write every single day of the week. You need break time,
personal time, and family time. Although I sometimes have to,
I prefer not to write on weekends. This is the precious time I
spend with my husband, with our family and friends, and in
my rose garden. I try to build into any writing schedule some
cushion time. Writers get the flu, have unexpected delays,
have to wait for information or an interview, and generally
must cope with life. So when working on my schedule, I
regularly add another month to the time I believe it will take
me to complete any book project.

Research will take you longer than you want to admit. On a
big book, such as *What to Do When a Loved One Dies*
(Dickens Press), which is about 200,000 words long, the
research took two months. This is the reading, talking-to-
experts, and digging-up-information time that I really don't
enjoy, but is oh so essential.

Even before I began writing the first chapter, I felt like a
walking encyclopedia of grief management techniques with all
those facts and figures in my head. Plus, I had piles of
research and information that kept coming to me throughout
the writing process, so I had to go back into the manuscript
and make changes.

I am a fast writer, and when the research is completed and I
have a strong outline, I can produce between 3,000 and 5,000
words a day, sometimes more. We're not talking highly
academic or scientific material, but how-to books like the one
you're holding. Before you scream about my production-line
style of writing, keep in mind that I've been writing
professionally for nearly twenty years. I've got the drill down

pat, and everything from sentence structure to citing a quotation is easy because I've done it hundreds of times.

Let's say the book you're writing will end up at about 60,000 words with ten chapters of about 6,000 each. You know you can write a 1,000-word article in a day. It would seem then that the writing of the book will take you only about two months. Now add in weekends and cushion time — when you have to spend the day at the vet with your cat or weather some other crisis. Okay, it still sounds perfect. The book can be done in under three months. Well, think again.

Like research, interviews, and the editing process, writing always takes longer than you imagine. Just when everything is moving along smoothly, Mother Nature throws a blizzard at you and the kids are home for a week.

For a 60,000-word book, a savvy writer allows at least five months from the get-go to completion and adds another month for luck. Editors love getting books early, so you won't offend any one in publishing if you dazzle them with a finished product ahead of schedule.

That's an overview of how work is scheduled. Write a timeline for your project, and do it in gelatin, not cement, so you can change it when necessary. Post your schedule, just as you might while working on any time-sensitive project. Be tough on yourself, but do not feel crushed should the plan need to be altered.

Be honest. Praise yourself when you complete a portion of the work. Become a clock watcher. Your boss (that's you) is watching every move you make. Check out the information in Chapter 11 about time-saving and management skills for writers.

 ## Change the Way You Answer the Phone

If you're constantly bothered by phone calls from well-meaning friends, loved ones, or sales people hawking all sorts of stuff, change the way

you answer that gadget. It could save you hours. I
learned this early on after quitting my day job to go into
writing full time.

By sweetly saying "hello" to every caller, you invite
people to chat. By answering in your best business voice,
"Good morning, this is (put your name here)," the caller
knows you're working. It doesn't matter if you have a
squirmy toddler on your hip or are sweating over a nasty
old lawn mower that refuses to start again or scraping the
remainder of last night's dinner off the floor. On the
telephone, your first words set the stage for business.
Until video phones are commonplace, we're safe.

Don't get me wrong, if I'm taking a break and need or
want to connect with a friend, I'll call. But I always ask
if it's a good time to talk and my friends do the same.
They respect the fact that I work for a living, even though
my daily commute often means that some days the car
doesn't move from the garage. They might hate the fact
that I do not have to cope with gridlock like they do, but
they don't hold it against me.

I always answer my business line during the working
day. I want my customers (editors, publishers,
ghostwriting clients, and writing conference staffers) to
be able to speak with me immediately. And don't forget
that valuable advice that I learned from a colleague, a
motivational speaker, to put a smile on my face and smile
into my words when on the phone. No, people can't see
us, but they can feel a scowl. Although I do answer the
phone and respond to questions, I often let the caller
know that I'll have to get back with the answer. Then I
set a time to return the call.

Other writers let answering machines pick up calls or
they screen the calls and only talk with specific people.
If you prefer these methods, make sure that your
answering machine message is appropriate and inviting.
When recording your outgoing message, you might want

to include a statement such as: "Please include the best time to return your call." This indicates that you do return calls and you're a person of your word.

Self-Editing Techniques

Have you ever had friends, family, or teachers edit your work? Sometimes it's painful. Sometimes it's pointless. And once in a while, it's good. Most of the time the recommendations these people, including professional editors, point out are things you already know. It hurts when you pay money to hear what you've been telling yourself. Stop before you do it again, and learn self-editing tricks. I'm ruthless with my own work, although gentle with students' writing. You should be the same. That said, don't be so brutal that you stop writing and stop sending your work to publishers. That defeats the purpose. The following are my favorite tricks of the self-editing trade.

- **Read your work in various ways.** Initially read it for foolish grammar and spelling errors not caught by spell checking. You can probably do this while it's still on your computer screen. Then read your work again for content and to see how the words flow. I like to read my work out loud. If I trip over my tongue, I can be assured that my reader will too.

- **Don't stop to change a word or find the perfect way to say something.** When I edit, I mark the problem area on the manuscript with a *W* which means *What?* and continue. Then I go back to all the *W*s and figure out exactly what's needed. This saves me plenty of time and keeps my mind on the content of the manuscript, not my glitches.

- **As you read, look for flaws.** Watch for redundancies, overuse of words, memorable words that come too close together, and awkward or run-on sentences.

- **Look for strong main sentences and colorful word images.**

- **Be wary of your golden word.** If you've created a paragraph or part of your book that just glows, outshining the rest of your book (we're talking brilliance and the stuff of which Pulitzer Prizes are made), watch out. In order to keep these nuggets, you may make the same mistake I've made in the past: Sacrifice good writing for something that really doesn't belong in your book at all *just because you like the feel of the words.*

- **Put your manuscript away for a while.** Wait a few days, a week, or a month and then read over the manuscript with a fresh eye. You'll be surprised at the good writing — and some awkward writing — you'll find. You'll also discover ways to improve your work.

Writing About Emotions

Nonfiction writers must be able to express emotions in their writing. To flex your creative muscles and encourage the writing of emotional words, try this simple yet challenging exercise. Close your eyes and run your finger up and down the columns below. Let it stop wherever and whenever it chooses.

Write for five minutes. Set the oven timer or an alarm so you don't give up too soon. Do not edit as you write. Let it flow. With all the choices below, you can have a fervent feeling-fest of writing possibilities.

fear	*joy*	*zest*	*lust*
love	*fright*	*horror*	*greed*
rivalry	*envy*	*pity*	*infatuation*
delight	*malice*	*spite*	*guilt*
vanity	*pride*	*shame*	*indifference*
passion	*distress*	*ecstasy*	*resentment*
bliss	*loathing*	*worry*	*alarm*
conceit	*triumph*	*rapture*	*bitterness*

CHAPTER 8

Successful Interviewing

A person who publishes a book
willfully appears before the populace
with his pants down. . . . If it is a good book,
nothing can hurt him.
If it is a bad book,
nothing can help him.
— Edna St. Vincent Millay

So much is said about what a writer should be, but is a good listener on your list? Professional writers like to talk as much as the next guy or gal, but they've learned that listening, asking questions, and focusing their inquiries all help to produce better books. Smart writers know when to stop talking too. The ability to listen might be a writer's sharpest tool. Listening well is essential when conducting good interviews, which we'll cover in this chapter.

As you read this chapter, you'll find ways to seek out the right expert so you can listen and get information. We also describe how to ask questions that get answers. If you've never done an interview before, this chapter includes tips to make it great the first time out.

Finding Experts and Using Quotes

Experts who can help support the topics of your book are everywhere, if you just know how to find them. Most beginning writers forget that fact or think that they have to call in Sherlock Holmes to track down these professionals. Not so.

Some beginning writers start and end their search for an expert by looking in *Books in Print* (the multi-volume source that lists all books that are available). This is a fine way to connect with an expert who may have published a book, but the going is slow.

Let's say you find the expert you need, Bart Brown, and his book was published by Contemporary Books in Illinois. To contact Mr. Brown, you'll have to write to the author in care of the publisher. Letters routed this way often take months to reach the addressee. Once the expert, Mr. Brown, is contacted, he then contacts you, the writer. If you're in a hurry for that quote, the long time element is frustrating.

I'm not suggesting that you forget Mr. Brown's quote. There are times when you have to talk to the original expert and have to get fresh material. If time is important, perhaps you can find a published quote from Mr. Brown's work; then you can reference, in the text, the quote's source. For instance, if Mr. Brown was interviewed by *Computer Today* magazine about life in the twenty-third century, then it might be just as easy to reference the article, including volume and page number, than try to get in contact with Mr. Brown for an original quote.

Consider too if you need a specific expert's interview or quote or if another expert's two cents would do the trick. If the latter is correct, your odds for success are excellent. A reference source I find essential is *The Yearbook of Experts, Authorities, and Spokespersons*, published by Broadcast Interview Source, in Washington, D.C. The yearly guide gives a thumbnail sketch of organizations and experts who can, and want, to speak on everything from the Wine Appreciation Guild to the Vegetarian Society of Hawaii, with plenty of serious stuff on the economy, taxes, investments, science, medicine, and parenting mixed in. Your library should have a copy or be able to tell you where you can get one. You can also contact the publisher at (202) 333-4904, (800) 539-6683, or www.yearbooknews.com, if you need to interview an expert on just about anything.

Permission to Include an Interview in Your Book

You may need to get permission from the people you interview to include material from the interview in your book. Some publishers want you to send interview releases along with your final manuscript. Keep a copy on file after you submit the manuscript and additional material (such as photo releases) to your publisher.

You can create your own interview release form. Here's what it should include:

INTERVIEW RELEASE

I, _____ (*interviewee's name inserted here*), give my permission to _____ (*your name should go here*) to use my interview in conjunction with the book, _____ (*your book's title or working title goes here*). I understand that no payment is expected for the use of the interview. I do not wish to review the interview material before the book is submitted to the editor.

_____   _____
Signature   Date

The Yellow Pages section of your telephone book is a convenient, free source for identifying experts you need for your book. In the phone book, you'll find experts on everything from astrology to zoology. If you live in a small town, you may want to use the Yellow Pages from a major city, such as Chicago, Dallas, or New York, to access more experts. Your library most likely has phone books from a wide variety of places, or the staff can tell you where you can get them.

Get Ready to Become an Expert

When your book is published, the public will perceive you as an expert and, in actuality, you will know more about your topic than the average Joe or Jill.

Consider paying for a listing in the Yellow Pages, *The Yearbook of Experts, Authorities, and Spokespersons* (Broadcast Interview Source), *Radio/TV Interview Report*, and other publications. Then when writers need an expert, you will be visible and able to push your books in the interview or the biography that follows your advice.

The Initial Contact

When you telephone or contact an expert for a quote, be prepared to do the interview right then and there. That means you have your questions ready and written out. If you have difficulty being spontaneous, write out some of the background on the topic so you can give your expert a quick overview. You will also want to tell the person, if appropriate, your publisher's name and the names of other experts you have interviewed. Be sure to read Effective Interviewing Skills in the next section of this chapter, before you make that call or appointment.

I've called some experts to set up interviews who helpfully respond with, "Why, let's just do the interview now." Should this ever happen to you, and before "Well, I dunno . . ." comes out of your mouth, take this advice: Prior to making that initial call, figure out exactly what you want the expert to say on the subject. The expert will, most likely, want to know the direction of your interview; they are hip to journalists. For example, if you're theorizing about family life in the distant future, you might say, "I'd like your brief opinion on life in the coming years, well into the twenty-third century, for a book I'm writing on the topic."

The key word here is *brief.* This expert may have spent an entire lifetime studying a topic to which you're about to devote 200 words. You're in charge, so ask for a "news bite" or a quotable quote to use. Before or after the interview, double-check the spelling of the expert's name, position, organization, and special notes for the reference line after the quote. It might look something like this:

> "I think life in the twenty-third century will be shockingly familiar to family life today," says Martha Miller, Ph.D., spokesperson for the American Family Quorum, with headquarters in Phoenix, Arizona, and author of *Future Families* (Rodgers & Nelsen, 1999).

Remember, you might be turned down for an interview by the first expert you contact. Okay. You've been rejected. So, what? Join the club. Now go on to the next expert and try the same technique for the interview. If, by the fifth expert, you're still striking out, you may be: (1) contacting people who are not acquainted with the topic, in which case you need to re-evaluate how you found these people; or (2) the topic may be too controversial for an off-the-cuff quote. In the second instance, your expert may want you to fax, mail, or e-mail background information about your book project before being interviewed. If you have time, fine. Do it. If not, move on to the next expert. There are plenty of them out there.

Speaking of plenty of experts, it's a hard and fast rule of mine never to allow experts to approve of the written copy before it's turned over to the editor. Some experts will push on this and make you feel obliged to do so. Back when I first started to write professionally, I thought all writers had to do this, and I ended up with experts and other people I interviewed draining my entertaining copy of all the exciting, interesting details. Of course, hard and fast rules do have exceptions: If I really must have the expert's quote and can't possibly use anyone else's, then I will override the rule, but that secret is between you and me.

Why Interview?

If you write you will have to, at some time, get information from another person. Writing your memoirs or family saga? You'll want to interview family members about their early childhoods. If you're writing a cookbook, you may have to consult with a nutritionist so each recipe includes information about the grams of fat and calorie content. If you're working on a business book, you may have to contact experts in the field. With a historical book, you'll definitely need to contact eye witnesses of events, historical society staffers, and librarians to find information on the past.

An interview is a focused conversation. You ask the questions and the answers you receive will help you write your book.

The Interviewer's Neck Saver: A Headset

A telephone headset may give you an extra pair of hands.

An "Operator, can-I-help-you-please?" telephone headset will set your hands free to use the keyboard during phone interviews or to take notes in longhand. When you're put on hold, you will have the opportunity to do something more valuable than drum your fingers on the desk.

Check the prices at office supply stores. Try one out for a few days. Most writers find a lightweight headset is far more comfortable than cradling the receiver in the crook of the neck.

Sometimes the interviews you need to conduct during the research portion of your book are not included in the actual book, and sometimes they are. Let's say you're gathering background information about crime scenes for murders that happened at Coney Island during the last year for a book on forensics to be published by the New York Police Department. You'll have to interview forensics personnel, perhaps people who have witnessed specific crimes, and maybe even the roller-coaster operators and hot dog stand clerks. This background information will add to the authenticity and provide facts that are backed up in the text you write.

Stephen Blake Mettee talked with authors and presenters at various conferences when he began to visualize his how-to book, *The Portable Writer's Conference* (American West). He discussed his idea with some of the best-known writers in the country and asked them to share advice. Then he gathered articles by these writers and edited them to compile his book. Linda Sivertsen, author of the Health Communications book, *Lives Charmed: Intimate Conversations with Extraordinary People*, talked with celebrities and then interviewed them about their personal beliefs and inspiration. The interviews are collected in her charming book. These examples of interviewing are on opposite ends of the nonfiction writing spectrum, but both resulted in successful books.

Tips for Becoming a Successful Interviewer

Here are some recommendations I've developed over the years. Following my own advice keeps me on track and out of trouble.

1. **Get yourself ready to listen.** Even before you contact the individual you want to interview, remind yourself that you're going to the interview to listen. Even though you have been given permission for the interview, you are intruding on this person's life. Your interviewee is doing you a favor.

Many new writers believe they will have to pay to conduct interviews, but this is simply not so. Unless you're going to interview someone of questionable integrity, writers are not charged fees to interview others.

2. Make an appointment. Make that appointment even if you're interviewing the person over the phone. This saves you time, and it lets your expert know you're a professional.

3. Prepare for the topic and the person being interviewed. Before you ever leave your office, find out as much as possible about the topic or the individual you'll be speaking with. Nowadays, you can research many topics online. Depending on your topic, however, you may have to consult with historical societies, medical groups, or back issues of the local newspaper for material that's not on the Internet. Really do your homework, or you may end up inadvertently putting your foot in your mouth.

The story goes that a journalist was compiling a book about the jewelry of U.S. presidents' wives. He scheduled a once-in-a-lifetime-interview with First Lady Barbara Bush. After the how-do-you-dos, the journalist admired Mrs. Bush's pearls and asked, "Are they a new fashion accessory for you?" Wrong. If the journalist had done his homework and even looked at old photos in print articles, he would have seen that the pearls were Mrs. Bush's signature jewelry item, and fake as the day is long. When I heard this story, I thought about Mrs. Bush. Did she wonder if the journalist had bothered to learn other, more important, information about her? Or if the journalist could even do an adequate job? After all, he didn't care enough to find out about her jewelry, which was the topic of the interview.

4. Prepare yourself personally for the interview. If you suffer from sweaty hands — and we all do when we're nervous — a thin film of clear antiperspirant, rubbed well into your palms will stop that. Try it well before the big interview, however.

Avoid drinking too much coffee before the interview. You don't need to seem extra nervous, do you? And ditto for alcohol. I can put my foot in my mouth without drinking, and I sure don't need to take chances by having a drink when I'm jittery about meeting an expert for an interview.

Remember to eat and take care of other bodily functions. Sounds basic, doesn't it? But sometimes things get so hectic we writers forget this. Years back I interviewed a top television celebrity for a book I was ghostwriting. I did everything right and was prepared to meet every eventuality. At least, I thought so. So what if I didn't have time to eat before hitting the highway that morning. No problem, I thought.

There I was, seated in the television producer's office, speaking to a star I saw every week on a favorite show and trying to look like I really had it all together, when suddenly my stomach began to emit noises. Now, we're not talking cute little excusable sounds, but a gnashing, growling, demanding racket. My face turned scarlet.

The celebrity, a dear individual, chuckled with me as I explained the problem and how I'd been focused only on the interview and not breakfast. She picked up her purse and headed for the door. And I saw my interview disappearing.

Then she turned and said, "Let's get some food — I'm starving too. The commissary is just in the next building, and I'm buying."

Trust me, I was mortified with this experience and will not forget that most embarrassing moment. It was all the reminder I'll ever need to take care of myself personally before any interview situation. To shield yourself from such a humiliating ordeal, prepare yourself in all ways.

5. **Write a list of questions, even when doing a telephone interview.** This lets you focus on your expert's responses rather than trying to think up pithy questions as the person is speaking. Should anything unforeseen happen during the interview (for example, if a forklift comes crashing through

the wall or the expert needs to handle something personal), you'll be able to glance down at your list of questions and jump right back into the interview.

I always write out my questions. People expect writers to have them, and I figure if it's good enough for Barbara Walters and Stone Phillips, it's good enough for me.

 ## Interview Wardrobe 101

As we discussed in Chapter 2, choosing the right clothing for meetings with publishers and editors is essential. It's equally important to dress appropriately for the interview session.

Gear your clothing to the event and type of interview. Dress in a way that says you're a professional writer. If you're interviewing the director of the Surf Museum of America, in Oceanside, California, a crisp suit (with scarf or tie) will be out of place. However, if it's the director of the Smithsonian Museum in Washington, D.C., a well-tailored suit would be the recommended attire.

Check out your clothing before the interview to make sure you're comfortable. If the slacks are too snug or the collar of that shirt is worn, you'll be thinking of your fashion faux pas and not the questions neatly written on your tablet.

6. **Get the equipment you need, and make sure it works well.** I prefer a microcassette tape recorder that has small tapes, about the size of a cracker. Check your equipment. Do the batteries in your tape recorder work? Do you have an extra set in your briefcase for emergencies? Do you have a map in case the highway is ripped up or there's a traffic jam and you have to find an alternate route to your appointment? Did you get gas before changing into your grown-up clothes so that you won't smell like a gas station if the gas pump nozzle slips? Do you have two pens? Have

you packed your reading glasses? Do you have coins for the phone, money for the parking meter, a dollar for the parking attendant?

A few years back I was interviewing successful entrepreneurs for a ghostwritten book about women in business. I was especially looking forward to meeting one CEO because we were both members of a well-known philanthropic organization. She agreed enthusiastically to the interview and I knew it would be a great session. My questions were ready, I looked the part of a book writer, and I had no trouble finding the place, even though I'd never eaten in the upscale restaurant.

All that confidence was thrown aside the minute I tried to pull into the parking lot. The whole lot was getting a fresh coat of blacktop, and I had to turn my car over to the valet. No problem, you say? None, except I was going to charge lunch to my credit card and didn't have any cash at all, not even change. No ATM was in sight either.

Once the expert and I met, we hit it off. The interview went well. I got just the information I needed. And I squirmed and fretted the entire hour about how I was going to get my Mazda back. Finally, I knew I'd have to confess or never see my car again.

The expert sweetly gave me two crisp dollars bills to get my car out of hock. I moved from feeling mortified to laughing at how naive I was.

This does have a happy ending. As soon as I got to the bank for some cash, I mailed the expert two dollars inside a funny card. The expert and I have stayed in touch, and when she needs writing advice, she calls. And she has continued to be a ghostwriting client. No, I don't suggest you try this technique, and I've never forgotten that terrible feeling of not being properly prepared.

7. Confirm your appointment. This is one of my cardinal rules. Experts are busy. If you traipse across town or sit in traffic for heaven knows how long only to be disappointed because the expert was called away, you may twist an ankle kicking yourself. Confirming your appointment saves time and reminds your interviewee that you're a professional whose time and attention are valuable.

Triple-Check Your Tape Recorder

Triple-check your tape recorder before every use. They are not dependable and seem to fail just when you forget to check them.

Before I go to an interview, I always record on the beginning of the tape the name of the person I'm going to be talking with, the topic, my book's title, the date, and other pertinent information. I try to be organized in the things I have control over because there's enough chaos out there just waiting to muddle my efforts.

If you have to say that you've blown it, that you need to re-interview your expert because the tape recorder didn't work correctly, you will seem less than professional and most likely the sweat will be popping out on your upper lip, to say the least. This happens. Take it from me that it can happen even when you're prepared. Test the tape recorder before every use and you'll reduce the chances of an electronic blunder.

Before you begin a telephone interview, turn on the tape recorder and tell the person, "I'm taping this interview, Dr. Jones, and I've turned on the machine. Is that okay?" Wait for an affirmative response, then begin. In most states, you must inform anyone who is having an interview or conversation tape-recorded over the telephone. It's the law.

After you've transcribed the interview (converted it to written form), put the tape in an envelope, identify the book and the expert whose voice is on the tape, and place the envelope with your research material in a file or other safe location. You may need to go back for more material from the tape or even use it to prove that what the expert said during the interview was accurately quoted.

> If you use a hand-held microcassette tape recorder like I do, you'll also want to use it for making notes, such as when you're sitting in gridlock traffic, waiting for the kids' soccer practice to be over, or during other time-management depleters.

Near the beginning of my writing career, I was gathering material about people with unusual professions for a magazine article. I hoped the interviews could be turned into a book. Perhaps this incident was a warning that it wasn't meant to be. I was to interview a dog psychic who had been referred to me by an animal behaviorist. I called "Joan" for an appointment, which was set at her home for the following Monday. I planned for every eventuality and arrived wearing a sharply tailored navy suit, high heels, and a bright smile. I hadn't confirmed my appointment. The woman was a psychic. I figured she'd be able to tell I was coming. Wrong.

In response to my knock, the front door opened a crack. And through it I could clearly see the bright white incisors of a *huge* German Shepherd who unquestionably didn't like my standing on his threshold. Ordering Otto to the side and grabbing his collar to forcibly move him (Otto was very protective), the psychic pushed her face through the crack in the door. She was dressed in a faded, formerly fuzzy blue bathrobe, yellow and red curlers, worn sneakers with toe hole ventilation, and no smile.

After this momentous start, we got the formalities out of the way (and clarified that I wasn't with any government agency). Then as my expert changed for the interview I waited on the sofa that was thick with dog hair. I was well protected as *Otto stood guard*.

I highly recommend that you confirm all interview appointments. There are other Ottos out there.

8. Introduce yourself and explain your purpose for the interview. Do this immediately after the introductions because, contrary to what your mother may have led you to believe, you are not the center of the universe. Your goal is to get to the point of your interview quickly, but you must also make the person you're interviewing feel comfortable. Small talk helps.

Be aware that you may be the first writer with whom the expert has ever talked, and we all know how "odd" writers are — just joking of course. Seriously, your expert might not be comfortable, and awkward interviews are not successful interviews.

When I interviewed the spouses and loved ones of women who didn't survive their battles with breast cancer, for a book called *Diana's Gift* (Linnie Cooper Foundation), I often had to stop interviewing so that these people could compose themselves. I could feel my questions turning knives in their hearts, many openly cried, yet they bravely continued. Another time, and for a different book, I interviewed the parents of children who had been murdered by a serial killer. I asked questions about how they coped with the media and their tremendous shock and loss. As a parent, these heartrending interviews shook me so deeply that I couldn't face transcribing my own tapes and notes for weeks.

Small talk helps your expert feel comfortable and will help you too.

9. **Start by asking simple questions.** Although some writers and journalists warn that yes and no questions are fruitless, I use them to help my experts warm up. You want your interviewee to be comfortable in your presence. Move in slowly.

10. **Once you're into the interview, change the tone of your questions.** Again, you've written down all your questions before the interview so you're prepared for this switch. Ask questions that have to do with the senses, such as, "How did you feel the first time you . . ." "In your opinion . . ." "When did you think . . ."

11. **Your most powerful tool for getting a great interview**

may be silence. Periods of silence help you, and you need to design them into the interview time. Silence allows the expert to fill the gaps with valuable quotes and information. Feel weird doing so? Pretend you are studying your notes or simply look away for a bit. Don't be surprised if your expert is waiting for you to stop talking in order to give you insightful information or add details you didn't even know enough to know you needed. It happens a lot.

12. **Make sure your body language reflects that you're interested.** If your arms are crossed tightly over your chest, if you're frowning, if you're jiggling change in your pocket or twisting a lock of hair, guess what? Your expert will notice instantly and give you a mediocre interview. Smile. Make eye contact. Sit forward when your interviewee speaks. Throughout the interview stay connected.

13. **Take notes of what's going on around you while you're interviewing.** As you ask questions, watch the tape recorder swirling around and jot down information about the expert's surroundings: the color of the office, what your interviewee is wearing, any notable accent, anything that will make the person come alive when you include the interview in your work.

14. **Begin to wind down as your time comes to an end.** Then ask the expert *the* most important question: "Is there anything you would like to add, or other topics you would like to talk about, which we haven't discussed?"

    Without a doubt the expert has been patiently or impatiently waiting for this moment and this question nearly guarantees you a great sentence or bit of information to include. However, you cannot ask this question until the end.

15. **Leave a little of yourself behind.** Leave a business card or name and phone number so that your expert can get in touch with you with additional information or to refer you

to another expert to talk with. Let's say I forget to give the interviewee my card and the person remembers a wonderful detail about the project on which I'm working. Without a doubt, I'll never know about it.

16. **Remember your manners.** Send your expert a thank-you note, written in your very own handwriting, to say how much you appreciate the person's time and information. Good manners are always in fashion. Additionally, sending a thank-you note has a possibly bigger payoff. You'll be remembered. Should you need more information, or the expert needs a writer, or if you want to use the person as a reference or to gain access to someone in the expert's circle, you'll be in.

Become at Ease with Interviewing

Regardless of your topic, interviewing will be part of your work. If you're not comfortable with it, and it scared me silly for the first few years, then practice. When one colleague first started a book on adoption, she was petrified to interview other adults who had chosen to adopt. A naturally timid person but a good writer, she was determined to share the stories of these wonderful parents. She confided her fear to me, and I could relate.

I suggested she try out her questions in front of the bathroom mirror, with the door closed if anyone else was home and she felt uncomfortable. My friend took the advice further and set her daughter's colossal teddy bear in a chair in the living room. The author got dressed in grown-up clothes, including putting on makeup. Then she told me, "I wrote out my questions, positioned the tape recorder on a table, and did nearly everything I was going to have to do in the interviews." Everything was ready for a interview, "except someone to sit in that chair. I used a stuffed toy to fill in for a human. I ended up laughing at myself and my jitters as my daughter climbed onto the bear's lap. We worked on the interview together — all three of us." My colleague told me she smiled extra warmly at every person she interviewed as she imagined them sitting on the bear's lap, just like her daughter had.

Try those techniques or ask a friend to role play the expert.

When a Sandwich Is More than a Sandwich

The peanut butter and jelly sandwich is practically up there with America's favorites of apple pie and Mom. So for the next five minutes, describe the process of making that PB&J. You must take five entire minutes to do it, so jot down some notes before you begin. You can choose how to complete the exercise. Here are some suggestions:

You can go through it in steps, such as, "First plant a strawberry vine."

You can make the ingredients sound sinful or exotic.

You can turn the writing exercise into a poem.

You can put a protagonist (the leading character in a fictional story) into this sandwich-making drama.

Go for it, and you'll never think of this concoction the same way again.

CHAPTER 9

The Need for a
Book Proposal

*A professional writer is an amateur
who didn't quit.*
— Richard Bach

By this point you have heard a lot about book proposals. Just
in case you're still not completely clear about their importance,
get this straight: The proposal has everything to do with the
sale of your book and may be the most challenging part of
writing your book. Yes, you do need a proposal if you want to
sell your book.

The Unsolicited Manuscript Maze

The book proposal, once considered a nice, but not really
necessary, thing for a writer to do, is now absolutely essential.
Today, if you polled all publishers and agents, the majority
would say that they refuse to read or even accept a complete
manuscript. Yet hopeful writers still keep sending their books
to publishing houses, only to be disappointed with rejection
letters.

Imagine you're an editor at an up-and-coming publishing
house. You're one of the lucky employees in the organization
— you have an assistant. She's overworked too. Every

morning you're greeted not by the thought of another stroll down literary editing lanes, but by gobs and gobs of unsolicited manuscripts. An *unsolicited manuscript* is the literary term for any manuscript that hasn't been requested from the author or writer's agent. Publishing houses like Health Communications, the folks who brought us all the *Chicken Soup for the Soul* books, receive more than 400 unsolicited manuscripts each month; they ask for about 100 manuscripts to be sent each month. They select 1 out of perhaps 800. And still, that single manuscript might be turned down in the editorial meeting that truly decides the book's fate. Why? The author might not have the right publishing credits or background, or the publisher may have a forthcoming project that is too similar.

Most manuscripts are not suited to the buying needs of a publisher. For instance, Health Communications might receive mystery novels, nonfiction Civil War sagas, and cookbooks. These are clearly not the genre this publisher is interested in, and yet would-be writers don't take time to research the right publishers for their projects. The end result is that novices spend time and money and get their hopes high by not studying the field. See Chapter 10 for ways to find *your* perfect publisher.

The majority of publishers and agents are good-hearted people. Most have *slush piles* where they store all the unsolicited manuscripts. If the editor has extra time, the manuscripts in the slush pile might be reviewed, with the hope of finding a diamond in the rough and having it become the latest and greatest success story for the publishing house. Because they occasionally do get really great manuscripts via the slush pile, some editors feel responsible for the manuscripts and have the best of intentions.

When one editorial assistant recently started working for a large publishing house, she told me there was a storeroom piled floor to ceiling with manuscripts. Eventually extra staff was hired to go through this slush pile, and every writer received a reply.

Some publishers and agents avoid unsolicited manuscripts like the plague, and you can't blame them. They return the work untouched and unread, but only if the writer has included a self-addressed, stamped envelope. If no SASE is enclosed with the manuscript, it goes into the recycling bin straight away. That's one of the blunders novice writers make, but you're wise to it now. Here's more you need to know.

Proposal Fundamentals

Where do would-be writers, who haven't a clue of what it takes to produce a nonfiction book, go wrong? Some think they can jot down ideas or bulleted points from a presentation, add a bit of fluff as one might on a sales proposal, throw in some numbers, and turn it out beautifully on a desktop publishing program. They call it a proposal. Others yammer at great length about their topics and never get to the point of describing who they are and why they are qualified to write a book (and have a publisher spend money producing that book). The majority of would-be writers who don't get to publishing first base, which is having an editor or agent read the work, seem oblivious to the necessities of good writing and organization. They think they can be cute, clever, and eloquent, and they don't need a format.

Publishers, agents, and most people in the industry have traditional ideas about what a book proposal should include. I'm not here to argue the merits of this concept, only to make sure you're aware of the facts. I'm hoping that after you've rounded first base by writing the proposal in a professional format that an editor or agent will read, you can get to second base, having the editor or agent pitch the idea. Then you'll gain third base and have an offer made. Finally, you'll make it all the way home — getting paid to write your book. Baseball analogies aside, writing a good book proposal is as critical to the sale of the book as is creating the manuscript.

Whether you are represented by an agent or send the proposal directly to the editor's desk, your proposal must be persuasive. The proposal must be attractive, absorbing, and entertaining. Within the proposal's pages you must convince a publisher or agent that you are the only person on the face of this planet who is perfect to write this book. And then you have to take a step further and produce the components to make the proposal fulfill everything you've promised.

If you fail to convince the editor or agent of any of these points, rejection is the next step.

Your goal is to make your proposal so seductive to an agent or an editor and the editorial board that they would be foolish to turn your project down. But be mindful, this is a business where the bottom line is all important. It sometimes feels like the accountants run the world; to be sure, purchasing a book proposal and publishing a book has everything to do with money and marketing. (You might want to check out Chapter 12 if you're wondering if you have what it takes to market your book.) You will need to prove that your book is so unique, people will be flocking to buy it — thereby making the publisher money.

If you now think that writing a proposal is a literary feat of genius, stop it, right now. Sure, it takes time to write a good proposal. But if you walk through a bookstore today, nearly every one of those nonfiction books on the shelves started with a proposal, just like you're about to write. While it feels like an enormous task, other writers manage it, and so can you. Besides, the steps to create a marketable proposal are all here for you in this chapter.

Making the nonfiction book proposal compelling is a tough job and is not for the faint of spirit. The next few pages will tell you how, what, when, and why to do specific things to make your proposal irresistible.

After you've followed the steps described in this chapter and your proposal is polished, you should allow it to cool; that is, put it away for a day or a few weeks so that when you return you can give it a fresh read. The important next step is to send it to agents or publishers. Remember that *perfection* is the enemy of *done*. If you're working to make your proposal perfect, it may take you years to get it in the mail. Do you really want to chance fate and possibly have another writer sell a book on your topic before you even print out those pages?

 ## Literary Darwinism

We're living in a time of economic uncertainty. No news there. And right now only the strongest writers survive. That's great news for the savviest, swiftest, and most serious writers.

When the economy officially turns completely around (and not just turns the corner we're enjoying now), those of us who have stuck it out will be well entrenched in our field. Survivors? Perhaps so, and considerably smarter about marketing our writing.

Send a Query First

A query letter is a letter of inquiry written to a publisher or agent to ask if there is an interest in what you're proposing. It saves time, money, and false hopes. I always send a query first before submitting a proposal, and I recommend the same practice to all book writers. Why? When the query is returned with the positive reply of, yes, they do want to see the proposal, then the proposal moves from fodder for the slush pile to the solicited category.

In *The Successful Writer's Guide to Publishing Magazine Articles* (Rodgers & Nelsen), we talk at length about using query letters to pitch magazine article ideas. Query letters for books are even more important when you consider the time it takes to write a book.

To write a query letter, you must have a good handle on what the proposal will include and what will be featured in the book. See Chapter 6 for the bubble method of outlining. Composing a query letter during this pre-research stage of writing can take you a few days, a few weeks, a few months, or even longer. That's a lot of time to invest. However, writing a book could take six to twelve months. If you then go through the slush pile route, it could be a few years to find out that there's little interest in your topic.

Looking at the writing and sales process, a beginner might say, "I can't bother sending a letter when I've got a great idea now. I'll just start banging out the book and fill it with brilliant words. And besides, query letters are hard to write." I've heard this plenty of times in the classes and writing workshops I give. The reaction is understandable because it is fun to dive into a book project when the muse is in charge. But if you're determined to be successful, forget such impetuous behavior. Why? Query letters are cost effective and an efficient use of your valuable time.

A query letter should be persuasive, neat, and brief. You have about thirty seconds to convince an agent or publisher that your book idea has merit. Queries to solicit interest in a book proposal take only a fraction of the time to write compared to a book. Queries work, and yet there is a mystique about them that we will unveil. The query letter must contain all the pertinent points of your book, and these must be presented in the space of just one page. Here's an overview of the query letter.

1. **The Lead.** That's your first paragraph, the hook that will pull in the editor's interest. To work, it must have impact and grab the editor's attention.

How do you do that? Open with an anecdote, provocative quotes, surprising facts, or statistics, references to celebrities or news events, wittiness or exaggeration, references to dramatic events or common situations with a new twist, vivid descriptions, thought-provoking questions, commands to the reader, unusual definitions, or surprising comparisons or contrasts. Your goal is to produce one paragraph that conveys your book's topic.

2. The Second Paragraph. The second paragraph is where you include the summary of the book: what your book will cover. You need to answer the five *W* questions: what, where, why, when, and who, and the *H* question, how. Be clear. Use bullets, make points, and mention sources and/or experts. List nuts and bolts stuff. Include a working title, if possible; see Chapter 6 for details on this task.

In this paragraph or the next, give the estimated length of the finished book in number of words; make sure it matches the length of books in general that the publisher has previously produced. If appropriate, describe research, interviews, or expert advice, including who will write the foreword.

You need to sell yourself too. Why are you the best person possible to write this book? No clue? If you can't figure this out, you may not have enough reason to write the book. Here is where you explain that you're so qualified to write this piece that it doesn't matter if you've been published once or a zillion times.

3. The End. Close it off and move on. "I will be looking forward to hearing from you." Leave the editor or agent with something that's upbeat. Include phone number, fax, e-mail address, and SASE. Make it easy for people in publishing to get back with you.

4. General Tone. Always write the query in the tone that is reflected in your book. If a query is lively and filled with anecdotes, you're probably not going to make a sale if you produce a proposal and a book that are serious and filled with statistics.

With queries, success is just a stamp away, yet some writers refuse to make that connection. A well-written query letter is your key to sales. While most writers agree it could be possible to have a career as a nonfiction writer without writing and sending out queries, it's not cost-effective or energy-effective.

Make it your goal to produce the best query you can. If you wait for a stroke of genius, you could be sitting at your desk for weeks. A good query must engage the editor's interest while representing your proposal and book factually. It must leave the editor and reader satisfied. Regardless of your topic, these points remain constant. Here are the rules of queries.

- Always keep a copy of your query. You can save a hard copy or keep your query on computer disk, but keep it. You'll be able to recycle that query should you need to send the idea out to more publishers or agents.

- It's smart to help the agent or editor. As mentioned above, be sure to include your phone number, fax number, e-mail address, and/or send a SASE with your query. These will not guarantee you'll get a response, but without them, you've just reduced the odds significantly.

- If this is your first contact with the publisher, you may want to double-check the writers' guidelines of that publishing house, even before sending a query. Some publishers don't accept queries but want all submittals through literary agents.

- Follow through with the proposal if you get the go-ahead. Call if you have any questions.

- If your query is turned down (yes, rejected), it's inappropriate to submit the same idea to the same agent or publisher again. Pleading and begging won't work either — there's no exception to this rule.

- Even if your query is turned down, you might receive an encouraging letter or note about your query, such as, "Like your writing style, but would need up-to-the-minute research included in a book like this if we were to consider it." Proceed as you need to. For instance, you would resubmit the query with appropriate current research directions incorporated into the new query.

Pre-Address SASEs

I keep a supply of pre-addressed envelopes available to make the job of including a SASE in my correspondence with publishers more time efficient. (This is a perfect task to do when your creativity isn't at a high point.) I keep the envelope's format on my computer's hard disk. In addition to having my return address typed and centered in the middle of the SASE, I also print the name of the agent or publisher (in a small font) just below my return address in the top left hand corner.

This is a simple task that reduces organizational time when I actually send out proposals, manuscripts, and other correspondence. And when I open the mail box and see one of my printed envelopes, I know immediately from whom I'm getting mail.

Is it ever appropriate to query by phone or e-mail? As you begin to work regularly with a particular agent or editor, you'll discover whether that person likes to get book ideas over the phone or through e-mail. If it's okay, ask for a few minutes to pitch a project. However, to itemize your book's merits to an editor who may not even be interested is a mistake.

Telephone queries require organization. Write out the query, think of the answers you might provide to possible questions, and have all the information in front of you before you make that call. Be prepared to wait or to repeat your query to an assistant before talking with the editor. If necessary, leave your query on the editor's or agent's voice mail, and repeat your phone number and name twice.

Telephone queries are advisable when your topic is an exclusive, a new item, or extraordinary. But again, be organized with all the information before you call, or you won't be able to sell the idea, no matter how brilliant your query is.

The Power of the P.S.

Anything you add as a post script will be read. Make use of this trade secret to hit home your point.

For example, let's say you're querying a publisher on your book about your life as a *roadie* (one who travels before or with a musical group to accomplish all the technical preparations and make the performance happen). An eye catching postscript might be, "P.S. May I send you a snapshot of Mick Jagger and me taken before his performance at Madison Square Garden?"

If that doesn't get the editor's attention, little will.

Formatting the Proposal

Before you try to recreate the wheel, preview these recommendations for proposal formatting and procedures. They will help you get ready to write.

1. **Title page.** You will need a title page. The title page of your proposal should be single spaced and in a format that's clear and attractive.

2. **Paper and printing.** The proposal should be printed on white paper with clear type. Pages printed using the draft format of a dot-matrix printer aren't acceptable. Use a new printer ribbon or make sure you've got plenty of ink in the cartridge and have another one on hand when printing the proposal. Choose at least a 20-pound bond paper when you print.

   Continuous computer paper is okay, and for those of us with elderly printers, it's a time saver. Just be sure to remove the feeder guides.

   Fancy (read *expensive*) printers are a joy to behold, yet if your book proposal isn't well done, even the most high-tech printer won't help you make a sale. Agents and publishers want brilliant and marketable writing. They really don't care that your printer isn't the most expensive one you can buy.

3. **Page layout.** The proposal should be double spaced; don't use a space and a half or triple spacing for printing. Set up one-inch margins all around. The white space on the page is like the frame: You want a good balance between text and margins.

4. **Paragraphs.** Indent all paragraphs five spaces. Do not add extra lines between paragraphs.

5. **Sections.** Start the first page of each section of the proposal about three inches from the top of the page.

6. **Covers or bindings.** I like to buy paper folders with pockets — the ones used for business proposals — and insert my book proposals in them. I do not staple or paperclip the proposal because it is safe tucked nicely into the pocket of the folder. Publishers seem to have an aversion to staples – it's always better to paper clip a proposal together than to use staples.

   If you're thinking of binding the proposal, you'll want to double-check with the agent or publisher about this practice. Some don't care, but many are offended when a manuscript is bound because they can't flip the pages in the tried and true editing way. If you do bind it, make sure you've got $1^1/_2$-inch margins on the left side of the printed sheets, instead of 1-inch margins.

7. **Page numbers.** Number all the pages except for the first page at the bottom. Some writers put their name on the top of every page, along with the title of the book, such as, *Writing the Nonfiction Book*/Shaw. This is called the *slug*.

8. **Copies.** Never send the original of your manuscript unless you're printing multiple copies. Things get lost. It's better to send the publisher or agent photocopies and keep a clean original in your file.

9. **Enclosures.** Along with the proposal, include a brief cover
   letter and a self-addressed, stamped business-size envelope.
   If you want your proposal returned, also include a large
   envelope with enough postage to mail your proposal back to
   you.

10. **Neatness counts.** Your proposal must be as sharp looking
    as your words sound. You don't get a second chance with
    agents and publishers, and if your work has grammar
    errors, too many typos, or isn't sparkling clean, you'll be
    regarded as less than professional.

    Don't go nuts on this point and duplicate the proposal on
    gray paper, binding it in a leather cover. Keep your
    proposal clean and enticing and simple. Show the
    effectiveness of your writing and how smart it will be for
    the publisher to buy this proposal.

11. **E-mail.** If you are thinking of sending your proposal to a
    publisher via e-mail, get permission first. Some publishers
    go berserk when they receive an attachment to a document
    from someone they don't know that is a bear to download.
    My. Not a great way to make a good impression is it? The
    same goes for faxing your proposal.

12. **Response time.** It sometimes seems like forever. In the
    interim, work on your book, write magazine articles, start
    other creative projects. Read about writing, take classes,
    perfect your creative skill, go to conferences.

13. **Follow up.** If, however, you haven't heard about your
    submittal in a reasonable length of time, say six weeks,
    send a follow-up letter. The guidelines that you've
    received from the publisher will probably state their
    normal response time for proposals and queries. Some
    publishers respond in a week and others take three months.
    After you send your follow-up letter, wait again for a week
    or so, then call with a polite inquiry. If you're working
    sans agent, this will be your responsibility; if you're

working with an agent, you may have to gently remind that person to check the status of your book proposal.

The Contents of the Proposal

Here are the ingredients for a nonfiction book proposal. I've sold scores of books using this method, with a bit of tweaking each time. The tweaking occurs when a publisher wants specific information before considering the book. That specific information might be: estimated sales of previous books, classes I've taught, details about my television and radio appearances, or adding to the sample text I've included in the proposal. One of the publishers with whom I've worked wanted all writers to include an outline by topics in alphabetical order.

Before submitting a proposal, find out what the publisher wants. *Writer's Market* and *The American Directory of Writer's Guidelines* (Quill Driver Books) are essential references for this purpose. By reading over the entries and submitting exactly what a publisher wants, you will increase your chances of connecting with the right editor.

Book proposals are generally a maximum length of 100 pages. Some publishers and agents prefer far shorter ones. Again, this why you need to ask for those guidelines before you write the proposal.

A book proposal isn't a literary masterpiece. It is a sales proposal, your advertisement, your brochure, your communication tool. And it needs to be interesting and easy to read and understand. Here are the nuts and bolts for putting together your proposal.

- **Title Page.** Your proposal's title page (also referred to as *cover sheet* or *cover page*) should list the tentative title of the book, and your name and address, including your e-mail address. If you're represented by an agent, your agent's name and address go on the title page in addition to your name. Find out what format the agent prefers; some use title pages that are generated at their offices.

- **Proposal Table of Contents.** This is the listing of everything that is in the *proposal*, not in the contents of the book. Do not write this page until after you've written the proposal, because your ideas may change and the page numbers will definitely change.

- **Overview of the Book.** This is a complete description of the entire nonfiction book. Here you'll need to describe who the reader will be and why the reader will buy this book. In the overview you explain how you'll write the book and share information. This is your opportunity for a strong sales pitch and the chance to discuss all the finer points of the project. If it sounds like a commercial with heart and energy, you've done the job well. Don't include phrases like, "Every American needs this book!" or "Millions will rush out and buy my book," unless you can back up the claims.

Remember, agents and editors are not telepathic, and sometimes they don't have the time to wade through fifty pages of your writing to get to the really good stuff. Hit them with your best shot in the beginning of the overview. Don't hesitate to make points that seem to you to be really obvious. Tell everything you can to sway the decision to buy your book in your direction, including the experts you will interview, the individual who will write the foreword, and the research that will be produced.

You may also want to add details that will make the book more marketable, such as the fact that you're a public speaker who gives hundreds of lectures each year to audiences in the 1,000-people range.

- **The Competition.** Make a list of all the books that are in competition with your proposed book. In your proposal you will use this information in the section called *Competition*. In this section, it's up to you to tell why this book is better than any other book ever published on a similar or related topic.

You need to find out and then describe in writing how the book can get more exposure than the others on the market and what makes your book even better than anything ever created.

Each listing in the competition section should include the name of the book, the author or editor's name, the publisher's name and location, the publication date, and the price. You also need to include how many pages are in each competitor's book, if there are illustrations or photos, and special aspects that make the competitor's book good or bad. For each listing, write a thumbnail sketch of the book and then quickly itemize how your book will be better, different, more innovative, and make more money.

If your proposed book happens to include expert advice, celebrity endorsements, innovative techniques, or break-through methods that have never been made public, the competition section is the place to show how these things will make your book better than all the others.

You may believe that your book idea is totally different from any other idea ever created, but that's impossible. It's the twist on your book that makes it special. If you cannot find books that are in competition with yours, you're not looking hard enough. Every book has some rival somewhere.

If you do not include the competition section, your proposal will most likely be rejected. Once upon a time, rumored to be back in the dark ages, editors and agents had assistants who would scour the literary archives for competitive books to see how they compared to new manuscripts. Now that work is up to you.

Be aware that if you can't figure out why anyone would want to buy or read your book, you probably don't have a marketable book.

Checking on the Competition

You must provide a section within your nonfiction book proposal that discusses the competition to your intended book.

If you haven't done so before, go directly to a major bookstore and review the shelves, then inspect other books on the topic in the library, one of the Internet bookstores, and *Books in Print*, making notes as you go.

The competition section of your proposal is rather like a mini-bookreport. Here's where you discuss books, always pointing out how yours is better.

• **Table of Contents of the Book.** In this section, list everything you anticipate will be in your book, including chapter titles, if appropriate, and details of the content of each chapter. Note: This section is in addition to the Chapter-by-Chapter Outline discussed next.

• **Chapter-by-Chapter Outline.** Here you'll need to itemize the substance of each chapter. You can do it with bulleted points or you can discuss the material in sentences. Most agents and editors like at least three paragraphs to one page of condensed material about each chapter. Include chapter titles. Cute titles are fine, but ones that really say what your chapters are about are more appropriate.

If you're writing a psychology self-help book, for example, some of your chapters may include case studies, and in your chapter-by-chapter outline you may want to group them together. If you do group case studies or individual stories together, be sure to describe the one important example or lesson each chapter will provide; otherwise the chapters that have case studies will blend together and lack distinction.

• **All About You.** Call this section *About the Author* or *Author's Bio* or be informal and call it *What's My Background?* Call it anything, but include it and make it good. Talk about yourself.

This part of your proposal is normally written in the third person; that is, "Eva Shaw is the author of many books. She lectures at writing conferences . . .and so on." Pour on your own praise. No one else will do enough for you if you don't do this yourself.

If you're writing with a collaborator, each of you will contribute to this section. Strong credentials may be enough to sell the book.

This may be the section too where you'll include the list of your published articles or previously published books. Include any appearances on television shows and radio programs. You might want to discuss the organizations to which you belong, in light of the possibility of selling your book to these organizations.

Some writers like to include endorsements in this section too. Grand endorsements for you and or your company or the proposed book won't necessarily make a sale, but they can help an agent or publisher understand that people believe in you or your book's idea. Speakers who become writers often include endorsements.

If you have problems singing your own virtues for this section, you're not alone. Many writers find they don't say half enough about their background and experience. To get around this modesty problem, write this section as if you were a friend — a very dear and talented friend.

Explain your unique qualifications for writing the book, your incredible background, magnificent experience, and, most definitely, nifty connections. If you're writing the inside scoop on a Hollywood scandal and you happen to have been a member of the grand jury when all this was coming out to the press, let the publisher know. If your sister is CEO of the publishing house you're sending the proposal to, let that be known too.

In this section include, if appropriate, your academic background, whatever makes you an expert, and who you know to give this book more marketability. And if your nonacademic expertise is more important and pertinent than the "book learning," stress that.

When I wrote the proposal for *The Successful Writer's Guide to Publishing Magazine Articles* (Rodgers & Nelsen), my claim to fame was the fact that more than 1,000 of my magazine articles have been published. Obviously I knew how to write to make sales. Even better, I teach classes and give workshops on how to write and sell magazine articles. Everything else — my academic credentials and all the other books I had written — was secondary because I had turned myself into an expert on this topic.

If I were to write a book on gardening, I'd stress that I have a garden, one that has produced prize-winning roses many times over, and one that has been featured in *Sunset* magazine. My academic credits might be of underlying help, but my current study in a nationally recognized gardening program and my gift for concocting great compost would add more credibility than any academic achievements.

Take what you have in your background and experience, and stress how it directly relates to the sale of your book.

- **Sample Chapter(s).** Unless you've already written a book that received a Pulitzer Prize, you'll be expected to submit sample text. Editors and agents do this to get a feel for your writing style and also to see how much editing will be required to take your book from the manuscript to the printing presses. The more editing and clean-up that's required, the more money the publisher must invest in the book.

Some agents and publishers only want to see the first chapter, to sense how you set the tempo for the book. Others prefer to see a sample middle chapter. Some want to see three chapters; others will take an incomplete chapter that typifies your work. Here again, it pays to review the writers' guidelines for the publishing house and to ask questions. You may not have to do as much work as you initially think.

Organizing Material

It takes time to arrange the material you need to include in a book proposal, sometimes as long as it takes to write the proposal. You do not need to move through the sections of the proposal in the order listed in this chapter.

You may want to work on one section for a while, then skip to another part. It may take extra time to find all the books in competition with your intended book, so don't set up unrealistic deadlines for yourself. Shoot for a completion date that works.

Writing the Sample Chapter(s)

The sample chapter proves to the agent or publisher that you can really write. You can spout off until the cows come home about your writing expertise, but a sample chapter will assure everyone that you can produce readable work. Moreover, a good sample gives you yet another opportunity to sell your book idea.

Get a copy of the writers' guidelines of the publisher or agent, so you can submit exactly what is required, in the appropriate format. Most sample chapters are 20 to 30 pages long. There is a fine line between wowing this most important reader and overwhelming the person with too much material. Remember, if you're asked in the writers' guidelines to submit three sample chapters, that's exactly what you need to do.

Each sample chapter should be able to stand alone, yet belong to the others. Think of your sample chapters as long magazine articles. You may want to read about how to write a magazine article to get the help you need to produce your first sample. Try *The Successful Writer's Guide to Publishing Magazine Articles* (Rodgers & Nelsen), the companion guide to this book.

Your sample chapter must have a hook that includes a thesis statement. You need to pull in and keep the reader connected for at least three minutes. The hook is there to promise something or to tickle interest.

The middle of the chapter typically has subtopics that further inform the reader. Using the bubble outline method we talked about in Chapter 6, identify seven to ten points. As you begin thinking about the sample chapter, return to the bubble method and brainstorm what each subtopic might include. Select the best topics when you write. Make sure you fulfill the promise of the hook and give the information you said would be included.

Finally, the chapter must have a snappy ending. Briefly summarize the point of the chapter. Depending on your topic, you might have a summary box with specific points that have been covered. Perhaps you will include exercises for the reader to complete similar to the *Creative Aerobics* found at the end of each chapter of this book. You may even want to briefly sketch what will be included in the next chapter. This is the same cliff-hanger technique we would use if we were writing fiction.

Write the sample chapter in the language and tone that is or will be in your book, just as you will write your query letter and your proposal,. If you find the sample to be stiff, awkward, or flimsy, the agent or editor will too.

Take time to polish your sample work. Make it the best you can. Many agents say that the better the sample chapter, the bigger the advance will be. It's worth putting in the energy to make this part of your proposal shine.

As discussed previously, your sample chapter may not be the first chapter in the book. Sometimes the first chapter reads more like an introduction or overview of the book. If that's what yours sounds like, you might want to consider turning it into an introduction, and write a different chapter for your sample.

Select the best example of your writing for the proposal's sample chapter.

Proposal Additions and Options

Make sure that your proposal covers the following considerations.

- **The estimated length of your book.** We discussed how to project this in Chapter 7. As you know, the size of the average, and most marketable, book is about 70,000 words, or 250 pages. The length is indicated by word count, not pages, because font size and such added material as sidebars and boxed information can alter the page count.

- **The ways you plan to market your book.** Saying that you plan to appear on the *Oprah* show is wonderful, but the honest-to-goodness chance of that happening for the 60,000 authors who sell their books each year is about like winning the Irish Sweepstakes. Sure, you can include some pie-in-the-sky marketing ideas, but back them up with a real marketing plan, such as running advertisements for your book in the media bible, *Radio/TV Interview Report* (subscriptions to this newsletter are available by calling (800) 553-8002, ext. 408).

In the marketing section of your proposal, include your sales connections for the book. If you're a speaker and plan to tour the country, at your own expense, to sell the book at the back of the room, include that information. If your company is going to buy thousands of copies of your book for its employees, add this. If you're planning to call every radio station, television station, and bookstore within a 100-mile radius of your home and offer to do anything and everything to get coverage, say that too.

Because I also write for magazines, I always make sure that publishers know I plan to write articles and columns based on my proposed book's theme for magazines. If I have some definite media connection, I include that information.

Read over Chapter 12 to discover more ways you can market your book and add credibility to this part of the proposal. Remember, don't say you'll do anything that you can't or won't do.

- **The amount of time you need to finish the book.** Be realistic on the completion time. If you work outside the home and have family responsibilities too, and writing can only be done on the weekends, you'll need more time than someone whose full-time job is writing. Estimate at least 6 months to 18 months, depending on the depth of your book project. A historical biography might even take you years to complete; many prize-winning writers have taken that long.

- **More about you.** Along with all the above material, I include a black and white professional photograph of myself with the proposal. No, this isn't necessary, but you may want to go ahead and make an appointment with a photographer. Do not have a family member or friend take your photo. Spend the money for a professional job with a photographer who will let you buy the negatives. If you do not negotiate for the negatives, you'll have to pay a fee or get permission every time you want to duplicate that photo.

When you are ready to have your photos duplicated, call around for the best price or write to me at Rodgers & Nelsen's address, and I'll tell you where I get mine duplicated. If you have them duplicated at the closest photo lab, each print could cost you a dollar or more. Patronize one of the quantity photo houses in New York City or Los Angeles and the price is a fraction of that.

- **Your video.** If you speak at conferences or teach the topic of your nonfiction book, you might include with your proposal a video of you in front of the podium. If you've been on television talk shows, those videos could also be sent. But do so only if this is an important part of your book or your marketing plan.

Before you mail your proposal, read over the Smart and Stupid Submission Techniques section later in this chapter. In most cases, you only get one try to pitch your proposal. It makes sense to take your time and do it right.

Writing the Cover Letter

The cover letter for your proposal should be just a transmittal letter. Before you write and print the letter, find out the name of the person to whom it should be addressed. That means you'll have to call the agent's office or the publishing house. Sometimes it will simply go to the Submissions Office or Submissions Editor.

If you received a positive response from your query, address the letter and send the proposal to the individual who wrote to you. Make sure that person's name is on the address label. Write on the outside of the envelope and in large print: *Proposal Requested.* This may help your submission get to the right editor more quickly and stay out of the slush pile. Writing *Proposal Requested* on the envelope will tell the clerk who sorts the mail that someone at the publishing house requested this proposal. Of course, if any writer puts this on an envelope and it's not true, that person might be considered unprofessional.

Use good quality paper and black ink to print your letter and the proposal.

It's okay to pitch your proposal in the cover letter, but do so briefly. Let your proposal speak for itself. Be sure to use the title of your book in the cover letter. Ask for what you want — that is, representation from an agent or purchase of the manuscript by a publisher. Years ago an insurance agent told me she had succeeded during a tough economic time because she asked for business. You'll want to include a line similar to this: *Please consider publishing this book, or, Please consider representing this book.*

Again, you'll want to attach a SASE and ask that the editor or agent acknowledge the receipt of the proposal. This will not guarantee that you'll get a note back saying that your package has arrived, because some editors and agents do not do so. However, if you do not include the SASE, sure as shootin' you will not get an acknowledgment.

Conclude your cover letter on a positive note. Don't say, "If you have questions or can't figure out what I'm proposing, give me a call and I'll fill in the details." Rather, say, "I'm looking forward to talking with you and your reply."

Make it easy to reach you. Include your name, address, phone number, and e-mail address on the cover letter. Just as you did with your proposal and the previous query letter, make this cover letter clean and correct.

Smart and Stupid Submission Techniques

How and when you submit your proposal could have an effect on the outcome. Here are some tips.

- **Send it sensibly.** If you like, send your proposal by express mail or any of the other express delivery services, but don't send it by certified mail with a return receipt required. If someone has to physically go to the post office and stand in line in order to retrieve your parcel, you won't be making friends. Don't send your proposal via book rate or fourth class. Sure it's lots cheaper but the package may take weeks to even travel across town.

- **Bribery is futile.** Forget about sending flowers, candy, lavish gifts, and that sort of stuff to agents and publishers to get them to read your proposal. They may love the treats, but if the work isn't marketable they won't accept your book, regardless of the temptations you include.

- **Note your return policies.** If — horror of horrors — the agent or publisher doesn't want to snap up your proposal, and you wish to have it returned, always include a suitable mailing container and sufficient postage for the job.

- **Follow-up courteously.** According to an editor at one of the newer and more forward-thinking publishing houses, the kiss of death for a proposal is to pester an editor for the status of the proposal. Pester is the key word here. Send out the proposal (with fingers crossed, of course); wait the expected amount of time, based on the guidelines you studied before you contacted the publisher; and then if you don't hear after two weeks past the expected return date, make a polite call.

Post It Right

With all the postal options, savvy writers become smart postal consumers. Depending on how much mail you send from your home office, you could be wasting money by putting on too many stamps just because your packages and envelopes feel heavy. To save time and money, get an accurate postage scale for your office.

Weigh all envelopes. Keep in mind the new postal restrictions: If a package is bumpy or weighs over 16 ounces, you cannot drop it into a mailbox; instead you will have to give it to a postal clerk. Call your local post office for details.

Use a postal substation, sometimes located in stationery stores. They often handle express mail, but not international mail. Check 'em out if you want to save time. They're usually not crowded.

For tax purposes, get a receipt every time you use a postal service. If you buy stamps from a machine, write the amount paid, date, and location on a slip of paper. Keep it for tax time.

After your proposal has been accepted, ask your editor or publisher for the company's express mail account number to use when you send in your manuscript. It could save you some money.

I recently sent a proposal to a publisher I've worked with before. The proposal was scheduled to be discussed at an editorial meeting on a certain day and, in the wee hours of that certain day, Mother Nature produced a blizzard. No one showed up at work for three more days. The proposal was fine and the book sold, but there was a lag time of another month before everyone could get together again for decision making.

• **Handle rejection rationally.** Let's say you do everything apple-pie perfectly and the proposal isn't accepted. Hey, it happens. You can't take it personally. If you've done everything you can to bulletproof your proposal, most likely the agent or editor is simply not handling your type of book. Moreover, editors have poor judgment, bad days, personal problems, and family problems.

Some editors return books that would have been great sellers. Just recently, I met a well-known editor at a conference. Late in the afternoon over iced tea we were talking about the fact that even great books get rejected. She confided that she had had the opportunity to see and *pass* on (that means *reject*) *Chicken Soup for the Soul* before it was sold to Health Communications and became a publishing legend. She says, "I still marvel at my decision, but my reason for not accepting was good then: Collections of essays were not selling." She then remarked that she wished she had been blessed with clairvoyance. She was just one of about thirty editors who didn't see the brilliance in "soup" books. Here are some other famous titles that have been passed on.

Kon Tiki, by Thor Heyerdahl, was rejected eight times.

Jonathan Livingston Seagull, by Richard Bach, was turned down more than six times.

The Good Earth, by Pearl Buck, was rejected twelve or more times.

The Godfather, by Mario Puzo, which eventually sold over 15 million copies, was rejected by fifteen publishers before it was purchased for a $5,000 advance.

Doctor's Quick Weight Loss Diet, by Dr. Irwin Maxwell Stillman, was rejected sixteen times. It sold millions and became the standard for all weight loss self-help books.

Dubliners, by James Joyce, was returned to one of the most respected and famous writers of our time by more than twenty publishers, here in American and abroad.

John Creasey, the author of more than 500 books under various pen names, received 743 rejections before his first mystery was accepted.

My own story of the rejections for *60-Second Shiatzu* (Mills & Sanderson and Henry Holt Publishers) is right up there in this list of publishing brush-offs. So if you believe that you have a book to write or that the proposal and book you're working on is good stuff, even great stuff, stick with it. Rejection only stops those who want to be stopped.

- **Simultaneous submissions are expedient.** In book and magazine writing there's a controversy about the issue of submitting proposals to more than one agent or publisher at the same time. This practice is called *simultaneous submissions*, and you've probably heard about the flak on this subject that has been generated in writing circles. Some men and women think sending simultaneous submissions is next to breaking all ten of the commandments; others say, "Get real."

The consensus among published writers is that it's crazy not to simultaneously submit material. At the time you're sending out a proposal, you're offering the concept. *Offering* is the operative word here because you don't even know if the agent or publisher is interested. However, once there is a nibble that requires you to agree to accept a contract, then it's time to stop shopping the proposal. The simultaneous submissions of the proposal and manuscript should stop once you have agreed to accept the contract or representation. Of course if you are contracting with an agent, the agent takes care of this.

Sending submissions simultaneously is rather like putting your house on the market. You want the real estate agent to put a sign on your lawn, put an ad in the Sunday homes section of the newspaper, and make sure your home goes into the multiple listing, so other agents can get cracking too. It's silly to think that a realtor would tell one person at a time that your house was for sale, perhaps even telling someone who doesn't want to buy the house and then getting your hopes up.

Similarly, to make a quick sale or stir up interest in your book, you should contact as many agents or publishers as possible.

If sending simultaneous submissions makes you uncomfortable, get over it. It's the way business is done these days. However, be prepared for some backlash. You still may meet publishers and agents who think you should wait weeks and months for their feedback before you are free to allow others to look at your proposal.

 ## The Proposal Test

Feedback is a necessary part of our professional growth. We get it when a book or article is accepted. We get it with rejection slips too. Before you send out your next proposal, give it this test. Be fair with your self-evaluation but not ruthless. If, before you read the tips found in this book, you wrote another proposal and still haven't sold that book, run that proposal through this test too.

Give yourself 10 points for every *yes* answer, 0 points for every *no* answer.

<u>Score</u>	<u>Question</u>
_____	1. Does the opening paragraph of your proposal hook the reader? Does the material on your first page keep interest high?
_____	2. Can you identify the main idea of your book in 25 words or fewer?
_____	3. Does your book make a promise? A promise might be to inform or entertain a reader.
_____	4. If you hadn't come up with the idea for this book, would you buy a book on this topic?
_____	5. Can you list the ten most important points found in your book?
_____	6. Is your opinion or slant on the topic clear?
_____	7. Is all the material cited in your book accurate in all ways?

_____ 8. Are your examples pertinent?

_____ 9. Have you clearly stated why you are qualified to write this book?

_____ 10. Have you included the most interesting chapter as a sample chapter?

_____ 11. Have you reviewed, and in your proposal adhered to, the writers' guidelines from the agent or publishing house?

_____ 12. Have you produced the proposal in a format that's acceptable for the publishing industry?

_____ 13. Have you double-checked the spelling and the grammar?

_____ 14. Have you packaged it neatly?

_____ 15. Does your proposal give enough information to enable the agent or editor to make a decision about the financial benefits for a publishing house to buy your book?

Scoring:

120-150 points. Read the proposal once more and send it out, or just send it out again. If it's rejected two more times, change the title — throughout the proposal and not just on the title page — and send it to more publishers.

80-110 points. Let your proposal "cool" for a week, and then read it again. During this time, read books on your craft to gain a better understanding of the creative and sales aspects of publishing books.

70 points and under. Do more research, give the book proposal a twist, and keep plugging at it. If you haven't read the previous section in this chapter about editors and their mistakes on bestsellers, do so right now.

You Are 18 Again

Write the number **18** (not spelled out) in large numbers in the middle of a piece of paper. Circle the number **18** or draw a frame around it. Make the number stand out. Make it feel like it's an important number.

Now think back to when you were about eighteen years old. It's a pivotal age for most people. It's the time we finish high school, go on to work or college, or have other adventures and misadventures. Like other times in our lives that are marked with numbers, eighteen is memorable.

When I became eighteen, I had just graduated from high school, a B- and C student who had to work to make even those grades, but my family thought I was a marvel. My parents were raised during the Great Depression, and attending high school was a luxury their families hadn't been able to afford. I was the first in my family to graduate, and they were delighted. We had a little party in our backyard and the air was perfumed with flowers. I can still see the apricot-colored cotton minidress I wore, the Duncan Hines chocolate layer cake my mother baked, the balloons, and homemade decorations. Forgotten are the presents and the rest of the menu, yet the feeling lingers. Although there were many tough times growing up and even more to hit me head on in later years, the day I turned eighteen, I felt like a princess.

What do you remember?

For five minutes or more, write from the vantage point of memory about yourself at the age of eighteen. Don't forget to include the setting (for me, it was the backyard party). You have to be in one place for this exercise. Include the clothing you wore, the smells, the food, the fears, the loves and hates, and the friendships of the times.

For overachievers, do this same *Creative Aerobics* exercise every day for a week using various memorable birthdays or events, such as the birth of your first child or grandchild, the day you were promoted, graduation day, your wedding.

For extra credit, be sure to include dialogue that you remember or that may have occurred between the people in your memory.

CHAPTER 10

Publishers and Agents

Whenever I'm asked what kind of writing
is the most lucrative,
I have to say, ransom notes.
— H. Swanson, Literary Agent

Is the perfect agent or publisher out there for you and your book? Absolutely. Unfortunately, writers have been known to snap at the first offer from an agent or a publisher and live to regret it. You have a product to sell — your book — and an agent and publisher can help you do a more effective job when you select the right ones. That's what this chapter is all about.

We'll also talk about how to work with the agent and publisher you select, editorial etiquette, tips on how to negotiate a book contract, self-publishing guides and suggestions, and other options.

Finding the Right Agent

Literary agents represent you in the publishing world. An agent is your liaison with the publisher. There's a Catch-22 here. An agent is tough to acquire when you have no book-writing credentials, when you really need one. Then when you become ultra-successful, you may not need one, and they will be knocking at your door.

Most writers have agents because most writers (present company included) would rather write than handle book deals. Agents negotiate contracts, clarify publishing issues on your behalf, smooth ruffled feathers, referee when necessary, and generally look out for you. Your agent only makes money when you do, so it is in the agent's best interest to sell your proposal. When you have lots of contracts, sell lots of books, and make money, your agent makes money too.

 ## Paying for a Reading

We're not talking psychic readings here, but rather the fees some literary agencies and publishing houses charge to review a writer's work. Are the fees ethical? Yes, and sometimes no.

Looking at this from a literary agent's point of view, it makes sense to charge a small amount ($100 or so) for the time an agent takes to read a proposal or manuscript. About ten years ago, an agency house of questionable reputation was charging would-be authors a small reading fee. When the writer's check was deposited to the agent's bank account, the manuscript was returned, accompanied by a glowing letter that implored the writer to use the firm's literary service to "improve the manuscript." This would only cost another $500 or so, and then the manuscript would really be ready for consideration. Do you smell something fishy? Unfortunately many hopeful writers didn't catch on. Finally enough people figured out what was happening, and the agency stopped the company's unsavory practice.

Before buying time from a reading service, find out exactly what you're going to get. A more cost-effective method? Join a writer's critique group or enroll in a creative writing class.

How do you find an agent? Such books as *Literary Market Place* have lists of literary agents and are good places to begin your search. You can also ask your writing teacher, colleagues, and published authors about their agents.

A few agents charge a fee to read proposals from prospective clients. This is understandable; it takes time to read submissions. However, those who charge a large reading fee — say, more than $100 — may be in the business of reading manuscripts and proposals, not in the business of selling them to publishers. Unfortunately every year I meet a few new book writers who have fallen for this tactic. The scheme gives reputable agents a bad name.

Writing conferences are wonderful places to meet and connect with agents. They go there to find new clients, as well as for the free trip and hotel room in some exotic place. Agents are most approachable at conferences, but keep in mind that you won't be alone in this effort. Other writers are attending conferences in order to talk to agents too. At some conferences, you can arrange for one-on-one meetings with agents. When you meet an agent you like, and you feel your work ethics blend, ask about representation. You must be bold even if you're quaking inside.

Literary agents are marketing people. Their job is to sell writers' talents with the written word. They are not, in most cases, editors or writers. Don't expect your agent to tell you specifically what needs to be rewritten in your proposal unless you've sold previous books through this agent. More often than not, the agent will simply tell you that your proposal or idea isn't right for their agency.

The secret to finding an agent you can work with is really subjective. Some writers want aggressive agents who will shake fists, slam doors, and demand the moon from publishers. Other writers want the low-key or scholarly types. Personally, I have to be represented by someone who is assertive and ethical, with a good sense of humor, and with whom I can feel comfortable chatting over a cup of coffee. Fortunately, agents like this do exist.

Getting Answers

As apprehensive as you may feel about it, you might have to call to get answers from agents, editors, and those who make up the world of publishing. Just like you, these people are too busy too much of the time. They have tough days, and although they are in different cities and time zones, they also drive congested streets, get the flu, and wonder about life's purpose. When you call, make sure that if you feel snubbed you don't take it personally. Follow these tips to get the most out of all publishing telephone conversations and e-mail contacts.

* Know exactly what you want to talk about before you call. Jot down notes. Even the most articulate of writers get nervous or tongue-tied at times. This rule also applies to e-mail, because you might be tempted to ramble on and on or to cut the correspondence so short that your original intention is lost.
* Ask to whom your call should be routed. Ask for the spelling of the individual's name and the person's position. You'll probably need this information so you can send a thank-you note or direct your query or proposal.
* Be polite and upbeat. Smile when talking. Remember, people feel a frown, even through a telephone connection.
* Keep it professional. "Is this a convenient time to call?" "I only have two short questions and will need about three minutes." Or, "May I call when you're not in a meeting?"
* Watch your watch. If you say you're only going to talk for three minutes, make it three minutes. If you suddenly realize you have something more to say (or sell), ask if you can call back or write a letter regarding the topic.

Agents need not live in New York City these days to be part
of the publishing community. Many publishing houses are in
out of the way areas, anyhow, so it hardly matters where your
agent's office is. Just glance through one of the publishing
directories. Falcon Press, which produces oodles of outdoors
books and guide books, has its home in Montana. Oryx Press,
which publishes essential information products for libraries
and professionals, is in Phoenix, Arizona. Storey Communications, Inc., which publishes books that are in harmony with the
environment, isn't in New York City either, but in the quaint
town of Pownal, Vermont.

Some agents want clients to sign an exclusive agreement
that the writer will have all book projects handled by that
agency. Others prefer to work book by book and have the first
look at book proposals. I like the latter.

You can expect to have the agency charge between 10 and 15
percent of all monies collected on your book. Some agencies
charge for telephone calls, photo copies made of the contract
and proposal, and other incidental costs. Make sure that you
understand what will be charged to you to avoid surprises.

Contact agents with query letters, as discussed in Chapter 9.
And keep in mind that just as every short order cook knows,
sometimes you have to throw out the first pancake that comes
from the grill. The same goes with agents. Don't be
discouraged if the first agent you select isn't the right one.
Keep looking.

Finding the Right Publisher

Which publishing house is the right one for your book?
"The first one to buy it," say most hopeful writers. Not so.
The connection you make with a publishing house isn't a one-
night stand. You want a long-term, mutually beneficial
relationship. You want to have your book well edited, nicely
published, marketed thoroughly, and on the bookshelves for a
long time to come. You want it to sell well. You want to make
money. Right?

To find the right publisher, you need to get as much
information as possible. Such books as *Writer's Market, The
Writer's Handbook*, and *The American Dictionary of Writer's
Guidelines* are your first sources. (Please see the Recommended Reading List at the end of this book for more
information on these reference books.) And while you're on
that field trip to the bookstore, find out which publishers
produce books in your genre.

 ## Market Guide Smarts

You've just purchased the latest market guide.
It's awesome. Now looking at it, you
understand how a child feels who has eaten
too much cotton candy and hopped on a merry-go-round.

Market guides can be overwhelming and exciting.
There's so much potential. Where to start? How do you
find the right publisher for your book? How can you
know if a publisher is right for you by just reading an
entry? These are just a few of the questions you may be
asking.

Like the advice we might give our children when they
start something new and challenging: Just look it over.
Get a sense of it. Take it in steps.

Some people sit down and read market guides cover to
cover. Most of us don't have that much time or
perseverance. If we did, we would probably forget half of
what's in this important book before we finished reading
the final page.

Here's a map to help you make the most of your
writer's market guide.
- Read the table of contents.
- Skim the feature articles written by publishing pros.
- Review the index.
- Flip through the guide and read a few of the entries to
  understand how they are organized.

Now get some sticky-notes, a pencil, and a highlighting pen. This is your guide book. You may write in it, make lots of notes in the margins, color important entries with a highlighting pen, and turn pages down for quick reference.

1. Put the first sticky-note at the top of the table of contents or index page that has the category you plan to use most. This will help you flip back and forth to that category as you review the publishers who produce your type of book. If you're interested in writing for a number of genres, mark them the same way. You may want to jot a key word on the top of the sticky-note that stays above the page.

2. Using more sticky-notes, quickly identify ten or twenty publishers that appear, at first glance, to be right for your book.

3. With your highlighting pen, mark the information in each publisher's listing to which you need to refer. You might want to highlight the name of the publisher, website, or key words or phrases you'll need when submitting your work.

4. After following the steps described in this chapter, submit query letters or proposals to those publishers that seem right for your work.

5. Now write — directly on your market guide or using another sticky-note — the date you contacted each publisher and your book's title. You'll be using this guide throughout the year and may have other submittals or other book topics.

By now your market guide should have a dozen or more sticky-notes and begin to feel like a friend. Make it your writing mentor and refer to it for information and motivation as you submit proposals and manuscripts, and become published.

Once you've identified some possible publishers, contact the houses and ask for copies of their catalogues. Some publishers have websites listing their books. Publishers produce catalogues once or twice a year and list all the books that they sell. Most new writers never consider researching their proposed publishing houses because it takes time. But if you consider the investment you make to produce a query and a proposal, you really do want to target the most appropriate publishers.

Looking over the catalogues will also give you a connection to the publishing house so that when you write your query letter you can compare your intended project with a book they are already selling. In your query letter to the publisher you might even write: "Your book, *Ranching for Greenhorns*, is a perfect companion book to the one I'm proposing, *Cattle Branding for Beginners*." What does this do? It indicates to the acquisitions editor at the publishing firm that you've done some research before communicating with them and you know their market — both good attributes in publishing.

When you look at the publisher's website or catalogue, you may find that your book would not fit well with their line. What if you don't approve or like some of the books that the publisher publishes? Let's say your book is based on Christian principles and, although the house is listed in *Writer's Market* as producing inspirational titles, you discover when you look at the catalog that they lean toward metaphysical, satanic, and occult books. How would you feel if you sold your book to a publisher whose other books contradicted your ideals? It's worth taking time to find out. (By the way, several writer's market guides are now available that offer information about specific genres, for example, the *Christian Writers' Market Guide*.)

If you can't get a catalogue or find a website, and you didn't see any books by the publisher during your field trip to the bookstore, you may still be able to gather some information about the publisher you think might be right for you. Ask a clerk at the bookstore to direct you to any books published by this company. The store's books should be listed by publisher in a computer database. You might find out that you and the company are a perfect match. Or perhaps you will discover that you don't like the quality of the end product. It could be that the cover designs are ugly or that the paper on which the pages are printed feels cheap.

Moving Ahead in the Writer/ Publisher Relationship

After this research is done, you're ready to send your query or proposal. I recommend the query first, but you're a grownup and can make that decision yourself. Call the publisher first and find out the name of the editor who should receive your material. This person may be the acquisitions editor, the employee who is responsible for determining whether incoming projects fit future needs. If you can get the name of a designated editor for your genre, even better. Direct your correspondence to this individual.

Keep at least ten query letters and proposals for your book in the works at all times. Remember, this process is much like sending out resumes in a job search. A letter back to you from a publishing house saying that your proposal is accepted doesn't mean you will get a publishing contract. It means there is some interest.

Be aware that a few old-fashioned publishing firms still believe that you should not send a query or proposal to more than one house at a time. (Refer to the discussion about simultaneous submissions in Chapter 9.) Would you limit yourself to sending one resume to one prospective employer if you were looking for a job? I don't think so. Just make sure that all your letters are customized for each publisher. Keep records on which publishing houses have what and the status of each proposal.

It's always flattering to get an offer on your book — that's why you've submitted it to a publishing house. Your goal, however, is to find one publisher that reflects your own ethics, hopes, and dreams for the book.

I have had books published by big players in the industry,
such as Random House, Prentice Hall, Crown Publishers,
Contemporary Books, and Rodale Press. These companies
have clout with book distributors and bookstores, especially
the large chain stores. I've also had extremely positive
experiences with tiny publishing firms where I'm definitely
considered a big fish. I like being able to call my editor by
first name and have the editor know who I am immediately,
without an explanation such as, "I'm one of your authors, ah,
um, do you remember such-and-such a book?"

Having a big publishing house publish your book gives you
a feeling of status. I've had some phenomenal experiences
writing books that have been published by large publishers. At
one, the editor not only adored my book but recommended me
for other projects that her editorial board suggested. When I
was in New York, she took me to lunch and afternoon tea and
treated me as if I were the most important writer on the planet.
When she became the senior editor for another big house, she
continued to refer me to her editorial board. Plus, the
publishing house did a bang-up job producing the book.

It's great for the ego and you can flaunt getting published by
a big house to friends and family, who might not appreciate the
merits of a small, lesser-known publisher. However, writers
can get lost in the crowd. A writer I talked with not long ago
was told to forget about doing any marketing herself because
all the marketing was done in New York, where the publisher
was located. Sounds great, right? Wrong. Even though my
colleague has written a fine book, it isn't a mega-seller and
she's not a celebrity, so no extra effort is being made by the
marketing people.

I recently called one of my publishers, a big firm, to buy
more copies of a reference book I wrote. My editor is no
longer with the company, nor is her assistant. The representa-
tive in the sales department couldn't find a listing for my book,
and they didn't even pretend to know who I was. I knew the
book was in print because I had recently seen it at a bookstore.
I finally gave the clerk the ISBN (international serial book

number). I placed an order for a sizable quantity because I give the books away as samples of my work. I had to call twice more when the order didn't arrive. As of the day I finished writing this book, I still did not have copies of my own book from this publisher. Would this have happened with a smaller publisher? That's doubtful.

Having a Happy "Marriage"

Contracting with an agent and a publisher is much like saying "I do" during a wedding ceremony, except there is no love between the parties involved. To make your marriage successful, you have to work at it. Here are some suggestions:

1. **Keep your promises.** And remind those involved if their promises are not met.

2. **Meet all your deadlines.**

3. **Produce the book that you've proposed.**

4. **Be willing to compromise.** You'll have to give 150 percent (just like in a marriage) and be willing to overlook the problems that arise, because they will.

5. **Work like your book is going to be a bestseller.** Expect your publisher and agent to do so too.

6. **Be available.** Return phone calls and e-mail.

7. **Follow up on suggestions.** Make the changes that need to be done.

8. **Promote your book** *forever.* Or until it goes out of print.

9. **Help your publisher.** See Chapter 12 on ways to help your publisher help you make your book the best thing since pockets.

10. **Don't be a pest.** You'll get used to being on pins and needles about editorial decision-making, take my word for it. However, no matter how anxious you are, calling agents

and publishers more than is necessary will not endear you to them. As one editorial assistant just told me, if a writer badgers the department to check on the status of a proposal, it could be the kiss of death to the chances of that house publishing that book.

Editorial Etiquette

If Miss Manners or Emily Post had given writers a manual on editorial etiquette, we might not feel so perplexed about what is proper and what is not. However, to get you thinking in this direction, keep these recommendations in mind.

- You get only one shot with a publisher on a book submission, unless the editor has specifically recommended certain changes and suggests that you resubmit the proposal or manuscript. If your proposal or manuscript is rejected, it's futile to send the very same material back three months later. However, if you sent it to the wrong editor (for example, to the educational book editor instead of the home decorating editor), it is appropriate to resubmit it.

- If you change literary agents while a book is being marketed to publishers, be truthful with the new agent. Tell the agent where the proposal or manuscript has been marketed, what transpired with each publisher, and why you changed agencies.

- Forego the temptation to tell your new agent that your former agent — that #$$#! — isn't fit to shine an editorial assistant's shoes. A difference of opinion, a change in your literary direction, and the time to find a more aggressive (cultured, persistent, etc.) agency are all acceptable reasons to change. Once you and the new agent become chums, only then might you cautiously display whatever dirty laundry is pertinent to the relationship, although I rarely recommend doing this. Until a time when you and the agent are best friends, mum's the word.

Okay, You Are Not Going to Make the Deadline

The deadline is approaching like a runaway freight train and you're tied to the track. You'll never make the deadline.

When you think you're going to need an extension, double-check your work load, see if you can delegate nonwriting work, and then figure out how to streamline your writing process. If you have no doubt you're going to miss the deadline, call the editor or your literary agent. It's more professional to shriek "uncle" two months before a book is expected than on the actual date the book is due, and you're still five chapters from finishing.

Even a well-thought-out and truthful excuse probably won't help. However, explain what has transpired, that is, Typhoon Buffy ate your house, your hard drive had an excruciating death (no, you didn't keep a backup, yes, of course that was foolish), you're just recovering from that second frontal lobotomy.

Before you make the call, find a solution. You might be surprised at how quickly your agent or editor shifts from expressing sympathy to demanding to know how you're planning to solve this snafu.

Keep in mind that supplying the manuscript late may well void your contract, and you'll be expected to return the advance. Even your wonderful, kind, and gentle editor could get angry. Go back to the beginning of this book and reread all the steps that take place in the book production process to avoid this calamity.

The adage is: Don't cut your corners, always give yourself some cushion, and work like crazy, if necessary, to be as good as your word.

- If a query is rejected by an editor, but a note is attached saying you should submit it again in six months, mark your calendar and do so, unless you've sold the book. You may want to follow up with a note or phone call asking if their list of books is full or if the house is changing direction on their topics. Try to find out why you've been asked to wait, yet don't stop sending queries out to others.

- When a publisher produces something you especially like, write a fan letter to the editor, the author, and the publisher. Too often we quickly point out wrongdoing; take time to praise.

- Read the entries in *Publisher's Weekly*, *Writer's Digest*, *The Writer*, and the other writer's trade journals and books to keep on top of where editors are working. Editors often move from one publishing house to another, and you'll want to stay in contact with your favorites. It's good business to send a note acknowledging the change or promotion.

7 Tips You Need Before You Hit the *Send* Button

As more editors, publishers, and writers use the Internet, lots of us wonder if there are rules to this on-line system of communication. The answer is yes. Here are seven tips to use before you hit the *send* button.

1. Double check spelling, grammar, and format of your e-query (*e* means *electronic*) before sending it. Once you hit that button, there's no going back. You may want to print out your e-query before you send it.
2. When sending an e-query, include your phone number, your physical address, and other information that makes it easy for the editor to find you.
3. Format an e-query as you would a normal query letter. While e-mail is less formal, it's still not good form to begin your letter with, "Hi editor." Keep in mind that this

e-mail represents you, the professional writer. Save those happy faces and other cute stuff for e-mail to friends.

4. Do not assume that every editor wants e-mail or e-queries. Some do not and will want to receive your letters via the United States Postal Service. Call the publisher to make sure of their policy on e-correspondence.

5. Check with the editor before sending your entire proposal or manuscript as an e-transmission. Some editors do not like to receive long e-transmissions because their computer systems get bogged down as they download your work.

6. If the editor gives you the thumbs up to transmit a proposal or manuscript electronically, find out what software program they prefer. If you're using a Mac and the editor is using a PC, the file or attachment may not open and the editor will not be able to be read it.

7. Be patient even with e-transmissions. Editors who request e-queries and electronically transmitted proposals and manuscripts are often more responsive than those who contact you by "snail mail"; however, they are just as busy. After transmitting a query or long piece of writing, wait an appropriate amount of time — say a week or two — then make an inquiry. Be polite and don't wear out your e-welcome.

Negotiating the Contract

It's happened. Your book has received an offer. You love the idea of XYZ publishers producing your book.

If you're working with a literary agent it would seem that all the contract negotiations would be taken care of without your involvement. Not so. Agents negotiate the best deals they believe can be made, but it's up to the writer to accept or reject the offer. Your agent's idea of a fine advance might be an insult to you. Or your agent may think you should turn down the offer if it's less than what you had anticipated, but you may want to go ahead.

If you're working directly with an editor at a publishing house, you'll be negotiating your own contract. It might seem a bit daunting at first, but hey, I do it, and if I can, so can you.

A publishing contract can be an intimidating, lengthy monster, or it can be an easily deciphered two-page document. If you do not understand even the shortest sentence of a contract, it's wise to consult with an attorney. Contact one who specializes in contract, intellectual property, or entertainment law. You'll find listings in the Yellow Pages of the telephone book, or you can get a referral from a professional writing organization or perhaps from a fellow writer.

Should you receive a publishing contract and think you aren't being compensated as well as you should be, you can hire a literary agent to represent you. The agent may be hired to work on an hourly basis or you may want to sign on with the agency. Few agents will turn down a client who has a publishing contract in hand.

As a novice author, you will have less ability to negotiate than a seasoned pro. I'm not an attorney or an agent, and I recommend that you take the contract to a professional for help. That said, when I look over a contract, I try to negotiate for these points:

1. More money (it never hurts to ask).

2. A deadline I can make.

3. More free copies of the book. (Most authors get 10 copies; I ask for 50.)

4. The provision to buy books at a deep discount so I can resell them at lectures.

5. A promotional budget.

Don't feel bad if the publisher doesn't budge on various points; but do feel bad if you don't even try to get more than is being offered. Remember, a contract is just that: an offer. You are expected to negotiate.

Self-Publishing and Other Options

Self-publishing your book at your own expense might be the right route whether you've tried without success to connect with agents and publishers or never even considered that way as an option. Yes, self-publishing is hard work. Yes, it can be lucrative.

Years ago there was a stigma attached to the self-publishing option because the books were thought to be of below-average quality. It was implied that good writers would never have to stoop to spending their own money to publish books. Today, with excellent desktop and electronic publishing capabilities available to everyone, the self-published book can rival any book produced by a big name publishing house.

Many of the speakers, business people, and entrepreneurs I know routinely self-publish books. They would have it no other way. When they lecture, travel, and promote themselves and other products, their books sell like hotcakes. Some make more on back-of-the-room sales of books than they do for their speaking engagements. These savvy folks wonder why others don't go the self-publishing route.

If you decide to self-publish, I urge you to get a copy of Dan Poynter's *The Self-Publishing Manual* (Para Publishing). Be sure to get the latest edition because the field of publishing is constantly changing. *The Self-Publishing Manual* leads you step by step through the entire process. Poynter isn't trying to sell you a product (although his other books and tapes are good), so you get all the information you need to successfully accomplish this publishing option. There are many other books on the market about how to self-publish from start to finish.

Self-publishing requires some money, but more so, it takes commitment from the writer to do all the clerical and promotional tasks to get the books to consumers.

Co-op publishing, or cooperative publishing, is another option. Some people join together to contribute to the publication of a book, pooling everything from services, such as editing, to financing. If you decide on this alternative, make sure everyone knows what is expected and have good written contracts for each participant.

Vanity or subsidy publishers (also known as *joint-venture publishers* and *co-publishing*) are an option you may have heard of. More than 10,000 books are published this way each year. You can locate a vanity or subsidy publisher in one of the ads in writers' magazines or go online to search them out. Some advertise in the Yellow Pages. Be wary, though. Vanity publishers have been known to publish anything, regardless of quality.

With this option, you, the author, invest money to have your book published. With most agreements, you pay the full publishing cost (that's more than the printing bill, to be sure, and might include advertising and shipping). You will receive 40 percent of the retail price of the books that are sold. With most companies, you must guarantee that you will buy a certain number of books.

 ## Safeguard Your Reputation

Work that is shoddy, unprofessional, incorrect, plagiarized — well, you get the picture — has been the undoing of some great writers. Every once in a while we hear about the aftermath of such incidents.

As they say in the barbering trade, you're only as good as your last haircut. Choose the types of books you care to write, and write with care. Know that it takes time to build a career and a reputation. Remember what the great philosopher Spike Lee said, "Do the right thing."

Write and promote your book as if failure isn't an option and it won't be.

While you might be flattered that a subsidy publisher is willing and seems anxious to make your book come alive, be careful. Consider the expenses involved before you sign any contract. You may want to ask for the firm's references and see samples of work. Ask lots of consumer-style questions and call the Better Business Bureau in the city in which the firm is located to check about possible complaints.

Go into this option with your eyes open because there are wonderful publishing houses waiting for and wanting your book. Sure, you may get rejected a few times, or even 49 times as I did with *60-Second Shiaztu* (Mills & Sanderson and Henry Holt Publishers). However, be assured if you choose to go with a traditional royalty publisher, you will find the right one for your book.

I Learned It Myself

For the next five minutes, write about something you taught yourself to do. Set an alarm or the kitchen timer, and tell why you wanted to learn it in the first place. Describe how you went about learning it. Explain what you learned from the learning process. Make sure you include why or how learning this thing affected you. Here are the rules:

1. Give it a title.

2. Start the first paragraph with a question or a quote from a famous individual. (Questions instantly hook the reader. Quotes get people to notice what you're saying.)

3. Use the middle to describe the who, what, when, why, where, and how of the experience.

4. Sum up the piece by rewriting your opening paragraph.

5. Read it out loud. Savor your words.

CHAPTER 11

The Stress and Joys of Writing

Just remember, you don't have to be
what they want you to be.
— Muhammad Ali

By now you've gotten a crash course in what it takes to be a
nonfiction book writer. There's lots of work, and there's
plenty of joy. To be truthful, you still need some more
information to succeed. In this chapter we'll debunk some
theories about obstacles to creativity. You'll find time-
management tips, ways to cope with the notions of rejection
and failure, suggestions on how to stay positive and connected,
and methods to really make the most of your time at book
groups and conferences. If your writing room or office needs a
makeover, you'll find information on that in this chapter too.

Managing Creative Obstacles

Every writer has personal hurdles. Some are real, some
aren't. Never make light of your obstacles: If they get in your
creative way, they are a concern. It takes courage to get
through creative Gobi Deserts, but when you find your way out
and dust off your britches, you know you can do anything.

Yes or no: Is writer's block a hoax perpetuated by people who hound the pages of a dictionary for just the right word? Is it an excuse for those who talk about writing . . . but only talk? Is it a creative recess necessary to produce ingenious thoughts?

 ## Stuck for an Example

You're writing along and it's time to give an example to illustrate your point. Don't fret, take a break.

When you're working on text, it can be a challenge to change from hard facts and information to something that will speak directly to the reader. However, contemporary nonfiction calls for these anecdotes.

Rather than floundering and grumbling, get up from your desk. Walk around and have a glass of water. Let your mind relax a bit and stop concentrating. An example will come.

Or do what I do at times when I have a surplus of information, and I can't find a creative neutron that is not consumed with the topic. Just make a mark on the manuscript that means you need to come back. I use two asterisks. When I'm ready with an appropriate example, I use the word-processing program's *Search* function to find the ** and I can get right back to that spot in the manuscript.

You can also use *Add here* or another identifying phrase. But I'm a low-tech woman and I like to keep the search simple. The next day it is far easier to remember to search for asterisks than to look for the exact words from your final sentence typed the previous day.

Basically, writer's block can be any of those situations and more. When you cannot write, nine times out of ten other things are going on in your life to stop or slow the creative process. If the water heater has been making a terrible racket, the dog has just rolled in something questionable and duplicated the behavior on your new carpet, and the kids are down with strep throat, guess what? It's going to be nearly impossible to write. If you manage it, don't count on your work being any good.

Seriously, if you're dealing with problems that produce mental, physical, or emotional distractions for you or someone close to you, and you cannot write, believing you are blocked, my best guess is that stress has stopped you. After all the dust settles, you'll find the muse and continue to write. Why flagellate yourself when it's only life pulling your strings?

A student in one of my recent book-writing classes was a third-grade teacher who was determined to write. She came to me at the beginning of the fourth meeting, crying. We walked outside the classroom, and she poured out the trauma. "You may want to fail me," she began and in a sob continued, "I can't write. I must be a terrible writer. I sit down to do the homework and the baby cries or the contractor who is renovating the house comes in to ask a question or I have to get lessons ready for the next day or my husband needs to talk about something. I'm just wasting your time being in class — I have a terrible case of writer's block."

After I handed her a tissue, we talked about her situation. No, I would not fail her, and no, she wasn't wasting time in the class. She just needed a dose of honesty. It simply was impossible for her to write right then, and it would have been for any normal person facing that much on her plate. I urged her to stay in class as much as she could, to learn, to soak up the how-tos and when she was ready, the information on book writing would come back. If you're in this situation where life is interrupting your flow, read everything you can about writing and your genre, and then when you're ready to write, you'll know it.

As to writer's block, whether it's real or imaginary makes little difference. If it stops you, then you're blocked. Here are some ways to deal with it.

- **Keep going.** The trick to dealing with creative slowdown is to continue to write. You can always go back and edit. Just get it down. If words don't come, get out of the office or your home for an hour, take a walk or get some other exercise, then get back to work on that project or another one on which you are working. If that doesn't help, begin a different article or book, or go back to your previously unpublished or published work. Read how you did it in the past, so you can do it again.

- **Go to the library for research.** When I stumble at writing it usually means that I don't know enough about my topic to continue. If I can feel the holes in my work, I can be assured that my editor and reader will too.

- **Reread or retype material you've already written to improve it.**

- **Write letters.** Include thank-you notes to editors, friends, networking contacts.

- **Connect with new or prospective publishers.** Locate a bookstore that sells writing magazines other than just *Writer's Digest* and *The Writer*. Buy some copies and become re-inspired.

- **Think like a writer.** Read books on creativity and your craft.

- **Make lists.** Jot down what is needed to complete this project. Then start at the top and go straight through the list.

- **Update your files.**

- **Send out queries.** Take some part of your book and turn that section into a magazine article. Send out query letters for that article. See this book's companion volume, *The Successful Writer's Guide to Publishing Magazine Articles* (Rodgers & Nelsen), to break into the magazine market and make some money while your book is coming together.

- **Organize your office and materials.**

- **Have a quick chat with another writer.** Discuss your current problem. Get the other writer's input.

- **Do anything that helps your writing.** This can include everything from reviewing a manual on grammar to reading books on dialogue and characterization.

- **Sign up.** And attend a writing lecture, a conference, a critique group.

- **Write at the times of day when you are most productive.**

- **Love your loved ones.** But understand that they may not be able to comprehend the creative changes that are going on in your life. They may be jealous too of the new direction your life is taking. Communicate how you feel. Make time for them and your work and continue to write.

- **Identify and stop the censor in your head that says you can't write or shouldn't write.** Bruce Keyes, author of the motivational book, *The Courage to Write* (Henry Holt), says, "Part of a writer's challenge is to identify inhibiting anxieties and devise ways to keep them from turning into blocks." Figure out your ways.

Time Management

Do you feel like you're tied to a merry-go-round and can never get off? The bad news is that you might be out of control, and the good news is that you can manage time better. The following suggestions may not solve all your problems, but try to incorporate a few of them into your life. Remember that any new habit — good or bad, including writing every day — takes six weeks to become enforced in the mind. You can change the way you manage your time and make more time to write, but you have to work at it and give it time.

The time of day you choose to write could contribute to your time-management success. Are you an early bird? A night owl? Most creative right after lunch? There is no best time for every writer to write. Many writers get up an hour earlier than when the family starts to stir in order to have quiet time to write. Sitting in bathrobes and slippers, they are at their most creative. Night folks reverse the process. Discovering the right time for your writing can be fun. This may be the only suggestion you need to write that book.

 ## Why Books Fail

Last semester a student in my nonfiction book-writing class asked, "Why do some books hit the bestseller list and others don't make it out of the computer?" Suddenly every person in that room needed to know the answer.

Books don't succeed, 95 percent of the time, because their writers have failed them. The writers get lost, muddled. Or if the books are finished and get published, the writers are afraid to market the books or lose interest in marketing them. Writing books and selling them is hard work.

Here are some of the reasons books never take off.

- Books fail because they don't have a strong hook.

- Books fail because they are produced in a confusing format. Construction, structure, point of view, or production are off the traditional publishing mark.

- Books fail because they lack an original twist.

- Books fail because they are poorly or inaccurately researched.

- Books fail because the writer rushes to finish without fulfilling the promise of the thesis.

- Books fail because the writer doesn't have the tenacity to write.

- Books fail because one or ten rejections stop the submittal process.

• Books fail because writers don't, won't, or maybe refuse to feel comfortable enough to promote them. It isn't easy to turn a writer into a salesperson, but that's exactly what has to happen to promote a book.

To understand why books succeed, flip those negative statements around. Work to make your book a success.

1. **Make a writing appointment with yourself.** On your calendar or desk reminder, jot the time and the day you have scheduled for writing. You would never miss an appointment with your doctor or the school principal. Likewise, you cannot miss your appointment to write. Because of other responsibilities, you might be able to have only a half hour a day, but that's plenty of time if you use it wisely.

It's easy to write using a computer or even a typewriter, but machines aren't really necessary. A pencil and a paper are more than adequate. Use spare minutes when you're not at your "writing place" to jot down thoughts and focus on developing ideas or on a magazine article based on your book's research. Where are these spare minutes?: While you're sitting in gridlock traffic or waiting for a child's lessons to be over, or while the family is watching a video, sports, or a favorite show.

2. **Organize.** Keep the supplies you need for writing in one place and make it handy. Not every writer has the luxury of an office. Many have portable offices and use cardboard boxes or plastic crates to hold file folders and their materials.

3. **Keep what you need on hand.** Who would go camping, cook a meal, or leave for a business trip without all the necessary equipment? Make sure your writing supplies are sufficient. Watch for sales at the office supply store and stock up on the things you use.

4. **Going to the library? Don't read.** Going online? Don't surf. It's easy to waste time in these two places. Get your real writing work done, and then give yourself time for a treat and a browse.

5. **Keep a time-management journal of how you spend a typical week, or even a day.** No need to lie about any of the details. You're the only one who will look at this. Your goal is to reduce or eliminate time wasters and the things you do not find pleasurable or productive.

Look around your home or your life. Analyze what's important and vital. Look at the duties you've undertaken that may not be crucial to health or happiness. Sometimes it helps if you write a list of the duties that *should* get done, and assign each a number. Try to maintain a stable life while doing only the top half of your list.

6. **Reduce distractions.** Let the answering machine pick up calls, ignore the doorbell, hang a *Do Not Disturb* sign on your office door while you're writing. Ask friends or family to call before a certain hour if they want to speak to you. Ask them to call before they drop by. Let others know that you'll return their phone calls when you've finished your writing time.

Hire or barter with children, teenagers (including your own or neighbors'), or seniors to take on some of the busy work that encroaches on your writing. Such tasks might include mowing the lawn, washing the car, cleaning the house, doing the laundry, vacuuming, and grocery shopping. No, the jobs will not be done as you would do them, but they will be done so you can write. If you have kids at home, trade baby-sitting with another parent for added writing time.

7. **Take time for your loved ones.** Go for a walk, visit over a cup of tea, go on a picnic, play board games. Do all the quality things when you're not at your best to write. Then

write when the family is watching television, the kids are in school or busy, and your spouse is reading.

8. **Think ahead and avoid extra errands that cut into your writing time.** For instance, buy an accurate postage scale to avoid having to go to the post office to weigh a letter. Get a fax machine that also makes okay copies to save some trips to the copy store. Organize before going anywhere so that you can cut down on the travel time and have more time to write.

9. **Don't make excuses.** You do not need a fancy office or hours of quiet time to write your book. If you write three pages a day, in a week you'll have more than twenty pages, more than 5,000 words.

10. **Learn to bow out.** When asked to do something you do not want to do, or you would rather write than do, say, "Thank you so much; however, I can't (you fill in the blank here)." Do you feel obligated to talk with people or friends regardless of the circumstances? Learn to schedule telephone and visiting time around your important writing schedule.

Do you accept invitations to parties or events just because you've always gone and yet do not really have a great time? Unless the experience is pleasurable (or you might find material for your current book), don't relinquish energy for the event. No, you may not feel like writing at that exact time, but you will have more energy tomorrow if you don't go to the party tonight.

11. **Turn off the television.** Do you find yourself watching television but can't find the time to write? Watch only the shows that mean a great deal to you, and hit the *power off* switch on the rest. You could discover two hours a day for writing using this trick alone.

The Joys of Your Own Space

Yes, you need a space of your own, a place where you can leave work in progress or materials in disarray. You need to set up a desk in a corner of the den or family room or turn a basement into a writer's nook. However, even if you're not quite ready to make this commitment, don't think you're not a *real* writer.

When it comes to a writer's office, how big and how fancy is determined by budget and ego. Pick up any glossy magazine these days and you'll probably see what your home office could look like if money were no object. However, money *is* an object, and authors are thrifty when it comes to furnishing their space, so don't think you're alone if you're not ready to furnish an office with top-of-the-line stuff.

Let's say you're starting from scratch. Basically, the best way to set up your office is to place the things you use most often near you. Keep the paper and the pens and the note pads at finger-range. The envelopes and stapler should be close too. I have my printer just an arm's distance away, so I don't even have to stand up to turn it on and print a letter or proposal.

A secretary's chair with wheels saves time. Buying the reference books you use most cuts down on trips to the library. A telephone with a long cord between the base and the receiver will allow you to walk around the office, perhaps doing other things when you're on hold. By the way, because I do telephone interviews to speak with experts from whom I need information, and interview over the phone with radio program hosts to publicize my books, I do not like cordless phones. It's been my experience that they sound fuzzy at all the most inopportune times.

Don't neglect the fact that your office must be a pleasant place to work. Hang pictures, put up a bulletin board, set a photo of your kids on your desk. An editor colleague who works out of her home discovered a way to accommodate her never-ending need for desk-top space. From a builder's supply store she bought a length of counter, in an attractive wood finish, about 28 inches deep, and had it cut in the length of one inside wall of her office. The counter is supported at each end by nice two-drawer filing cabinets. The three pieces cost much less than a good desk would cost, and the arrangement provides space for computer/printer set up, a writing area, reference books, and lots more. This was a successful, but inexpensive, solution to the desk-top crunch most writers face.

My office is simply furnished and nothing really matches in the sense that *House Beautiful* would accept. But it's functional, it all works, and it feels like home to me. One of the walls of my office is a floor-to-ceiling bookshelf. The closet is outfitted with shelves for supplies and I have two file cabinets for more storage. I spent a little extra on a comfortable office chair because I sit and work long hours.

I count my blessings every day. I have a spectacular view of my garden. Right now, there is a vase of vermilion roses sitting next to my monitor. On my walls, you would see framed covers of my books. They impress me and make me feel like I'm surrounded with success.

If you like music to work by, bring in a radio or CD player. If you need a footstool beneath your desk to elevate your feet, get one. If you want a microwave oven situated near your printer so you can have unlimited hot drinks, go for it. This is your space.

Add to the comfort of your office with a big chair to sit in while you edit or do research. Keep the temperature stable. If it's too cold or too hot, you may not really feel like being in that room.

Here in the beach city of Carlsbad, California, we do not need air conditioning because the weather is mild, except for about two weeks in the middle of August, when the air in my office gets oppressive. A circular ceiling fan has been a lifesaver when the numbers of the temperature and humidity match. It takes up no room, is quiet, looks attractive, and I can work with the window open. A window air conditioner wouldn't do for me; I need fresh air to write.

If you work at home, guard against using your office, even if it's only a desk in your family room, as a holding pen for the junk that has outgrown other rooms. Also, your office needs a door — one that shuts. As writers, we need privacy. Sometimes we need to be quiet to think. Sometimes, as when I'm being interviewed over the telephone, I can't handle distractions, and without that door, I would be far from articulate.

 ## Read What You Write

The title of this box says it all. It's the best advice around on how to focus and produce publishable words in your genre. Whether you're working on a true crime exposé or a Cajun cookbook, make reading time part of your work process too. You need to read in the genre in which you write. Constantly reading different genres can undermine your best intentions.

A writer of craft books was having one heck of a time writing a new book on holiday decorations. Her deadline was looming. The holiday decorations contract was her twenty-fifth book, so she obviously knew how to produce them. However, without warning, the book became clumsy, the language trite, and she feared she was washed up in the craft-making book business.

After weeks of hand-wringing and rewriting, the writer realized the problem. Instead of spending the evening reading about the creative crafting projects she loved, as she had while writing her previous books, she was reading one murder mystery per night and two science fiction novels on the weekends. Once she got back to reading about crafting and creating beautiful things with her hands, the energy and delight of her previous books returned. If you're having trouble writing, start to read what you want to write.

When looking for furniture, barter, buy on sale, shop the classified ads, and see what you can trade to save money on office equipment. Second-hand stores have wonderful old office furniture, including lamps and chairs. Paint and polish can do miracles. Watch the ads and auctions too. Companies with rooms full of great furniture go into bankruptcy and have spectacular office furniture and equipment for a fraction of the original cost. Ask other home-based business people to let you know when they upgrade the gear in their offices, and make them an offer on their hand-me-downs.

Become creative and remember, you don't have to have everything right now. Learn to make do. You can always set up your writing space on a table or a flat wooden door balanced between two small filing cabinets. The point here is, you have to shop around and ask.

If you're buying new office equipment, ask about the cost of delivery. Sometimes if you buy something else that you need, the furniture can be delivered free. Keep all receipts — even delivery cost is a legitimate business expense.

A Network You Need

If you want to write and sell your work, submit it. If you want more chances for success, network.

Sales people use it. Entrepreneurs use it. Store owners and crafts people use it. But some writers think it's not applicable to their creative efforts. Not true. Networking became *the* established way to do business in the 1990s and is continuing unabated into the next century. Smart writers access more work through this personalized method.

In your own neighborhood there are outstanding chances to boost your income with writing assignments and book-writing opportunities. That means you must tap into the markets for writing in your community, and let your community know you write for a living. How do you do that? By networking, getting the word out, joining organizations from Young Democrats to the Committee to Save High Street.

As your name as a local writer becomes known, expand your network. Could a legal firm use a workbook for the financial planning seminars the attorneys are conducting? Would your town's chiropractor do more business with some informative booklets about taking care of your spine to sell or give to clients? Have you thought about collaborating with a beauty specialist for a self-help book of beauty secrets? These people need the services of a writer — your goal is to let them know you're available.

On a national level, every time you talk with an editor or an agent or make a sale to a magazine, your network is growing. When you provide excellent material in a timely manner, you ensure your reputation as a serious writer. Therefore, ask editors for recommendations and to keep you in mind for upcoming projects. As you already know, editors tend to move from one publishing firm to another, and if you are part of their professional network, your name and phone number will go with them.

It's a fact of life that before people will refer you and your writing services to others, they must know you're an ethical human being. This comes across in the confidence you show personally, the integrity in which you do business, and in your professionalism.

Right this second, there are more than 250 people in your personal circle — your own network. These are the folks who tune your car, the checker at the store, your insurance agent and your physician, your friends and your college pals. These people are part of your network and they are potential sources for expert advice on topics for how-to books and articles, ghostwriting clients, quotes, and more. By letting these people know that you are in the writing business and asking for referrals, you will multiply your word-of-mouth advertising range, which is the core of good networking.

For business leads, as well as a weekly or monthly boost of professional input, join a networking organization. A professional networking association can be anything from the

Chamber of Commerce to the Rotary Club. They are excellent, although writers who work with magazines and publishers often understate the value of these groups. Attend a few meetings of various organizations, talk with the members, find out the scope of professions covered in the membership, and go with your intuition as to the right one to join.

Within an organized networking club, and simply by participating in the group discussion, you'll learn boatloads of tips from other small business and home-based business owners. You'll also have access to information from experts that could range from decorators to publicists, doctors to gourmet chefs. Some of these folks might need the services of a good writer. You can increase your income or barter for services by participating in a professional networking association.

Keep your business cards easily accessible. One writer I know keeps her own business cards in her right jacket pocket and a pen in the left whenever she is in a business or social gathering. As she exchanges business cards, that new card goes into her left pocket, after quickly jotting a note on it. She follows up on all potential leads before filing the cards.

Whether you join an organized networking association or network with people you already know, you must ask for business. That's as simple as saying, "Should you need the services of a writer for your in-house publications, I hope you'll consider me." Or, "I write (for a specific genre), and I know an editor who might be interested in a how-to book about your profession." Then hand over a business card and follow up on what you say you'll do.

However, you can get more than great business from your network. If you look and listen, you'll learn how to dress for success, how to approach clients, how to promote your business, and how to speak in public. Being around winners gives you the opportunity to learn winning ways.

Be a host, not a guest when in a business or social situation. Make others feel comfortable, and they'll be drawn to you.

Great Ways to Say Thanks

Would you like to cultivate quality referrals? Then you must tell people who refer book projects, proposals ,and experts for interviews exactly what constitutes a good referral for you. When receiving a referral, always acknowledge it. Here are some suggestions:

• Call and let the person know how grateful you are for the referral. Let people know what comes of the referral. Also, if the referral isn't right for you, pass that along. You need to clearly and graciously tell people the types of leads that you need.

• Send a funny and tasteful card. Buy them by the dozen — you'll need them. Successful writers always do.

• Deliver a treat: a bag of big red apples, a basket of sugar cookies, gourmet tea or coffee, a Dutch chocolate bar.

• Give the person a copy of your latest book or a book you've enjoyed and recommend.

• Call FTD and send flowers. A small desk-sized arrangement is perfect for both sexes.

• Handwrite a note of thanks. Start every day with a thank-you note to someone. It's a prosperity habit that's worth cultivating.

Give and you'll receive. As you become established in a network of writers and professionals, you must go out of your way to give referrals in order to get more. Why should you let go of any possible business when you desperately need it yourself? Simple. There's a law of the universe as certain as Newton's that says the more referrals you give, the more you get. This law holds true whether you're referring another writer to a magazine editor or a personality who you know would make an outstanding story for your city newspaper's feature editor.

As you receive referrals, always follow through by making a contact. Go the extra mile and follow up with the person who made the referral. Explain briefly what transpired. (See Great Ways to Say Thanks in the box on the opposite page.) This is not only good manners, it fuses your network together.

Networking is a 24-hour-a-day practice, and every writer who is serious about doing more than making ends meet should understand and use the principles of effective networking.

Book Groups and Conferences

As your career builds, become part of a network or group of professional writers. We're not referring to coffee-and-complaint clubs. I advise you to steer clear of the groups that meet for chitchat. Instead join an established network of working writers to share your triumphs, help cushion the disappointments, perhaps critique your queries, and provide instructional programs and workshops. At the end of this book, you'll find a list of national writers' associations. Contact them and get connected. Some are for beginning writers; others are for those who have been around the publishing block a few times.

Can't find a branch of one of the networks in your town? Want to start a local writers' group? Then do it. When meeting and talking with writers who seem to be on your wavelength, get their phone numbers and establish business relationships. When you call, always make sure it's a convenient time to talk. "Are you in the middle of a sentence? Shall I call back?"

Find a good time to network. You may want to structure the meetings, for example, by having prearranged topics and then sticking with them. This works well because you'll exchange ideas and tips on marketing and selling books instead of getting bogged down talking about local politics or the spicy gossip in the area.

Then take the next step and attend one of the writers' conferences sponsored by your national writers' group, or go to a conference open to all writers. You'll find a list of conferences of many writers' organizations in every May issue of *Writer's Digest* magazine and posted on their website (www.writersdigest.com). You can also do an online search for writing conferences.

When you go to a conference, make the most of your time. There's an okay way and an outstanding way to get the most from those hours. Here are tips to get the maximum amount of information in a limited amount of time.

- Find a conference in a location that's convenient and affordable. The cost of the conference may be tax deductible, but if it's pricey, that won't help you right now. Remember, you have to have some income from which to take a deduction.

- Check for hidden costs. For example, will you have a long distance to travel, will you have to stay in a hotel, are meals included, who will care for the kids or the cats while you're at the conference?

- Call and get a brochure. Check out sponsoring organization's websites. Read the material carefully. Some conferences are learning and educational events where published authors and editors come to mentor new writers. Others are networking gatherings, in which writers are expected to pitch ideas to editors and agents and learn from rejection.

- Who are the speakers? Are the seminars right for your writing specialty? I'd feel like a fish out of water at a science fiction or a romance writer's conference.

- What are the credentials of the speakers? Are they people you know and admire, writers you've read? Will you be able to talk with the speakers at a designated time? Can appointments for critique sessions be made?

- Why are you going to the conference? To meet fellow writers, to learn about specific techniques (like dialogue, writing a book proposal, learning about query letters), or to network with literary agents and publishers? Make sure you're clear on what you want from the conference, so you can choose one that will meet your expectations.

- Is there an agent or editor or noted writer you specifically would like to meet? If so, write to the individual well before the conference, saying you're looking forward to meeting, and ask if you can buy the person a cup of coffee.

A creative writing teacher, who had been seriously polishing a historical biography, took this recommendation and ran with it. Planning to attend a conference in the Midwest, he wrote to three editors and an agent from one of the big literary agencies and sent just the overview section of his proposal. "They were flattered (which never hurts) with the idea that I had written to introduce myself. It worked extremely well," he said. So well, in fact, he had two editors and an agent clamoring for the rest of the proposal.

- If you still have questions when you get the conference brochure — and you probably will — call for more facts. You also might locate a writer who has attended the same conference, who can give you a personal view.

Once you're at the conference, what you do will have a great effect on how much you get from it. You must plan your strategy. If you hope to pique the interest of an agent or editor with your proposal or manuscript, make sure it's polished and you include a SASE when handing over the material.

If you have the opportunity to sign up for a personal meeting, write down questions or have a list of potential topics of your work. Be sure to bring a tape recorder or make notes of each individual session.

Have your business cards ready and get a card from each and every person you meet — especially agents and editors — so you can follow up with a note, your proposal, or manuscript.

Before or the day of the conference, really examine the conference brochure. Plan your schedule carefully. Jot down or highlight the workshops you plan to attend. If two of the most desirable workshops are at the same time, arrange to get a tape of the one you'll miss, and sit in on the other. Ask for handouts at both workshops.

Network with other writers and ask about the workshops they have attended that day. If one or two sound extremely interesting, buy the tapes for those sessions.

Ask questions from the speakers and listen. Take notes. These talented people are there to be with you and share information. Speakers who are not comfortable doing so do not attend conferences. Be honest with the amount of time you need with the speaker, and don't commandeer other writers' opportunities to ask questions too.

Let's be honest. You're there to meet people, especially editors and agents. You're not there to hang out the entire time with people you already know. Here are some tips on joining a conversation group that includes someone with whom you really want to talk.

1. Walk up to the group and stand politely, but slightly outside, but not so politely or outside as to be missed.

2. Listen to what is being said until it is familiar enough for you to add a comment or your opinion. This should happen in about five minutes.

3. Within five minutes or so, there will be a lull in the conversation and one of the participants will turn your way. Trust me — this happens.

4. The door has opened. You can now enter the conversation.

5. A good way to become involved in the conversation is to first introduce yourself. Speak your name slowly and clearly. Then ask a question about the topic under discussion. You will stimulate the conversation, and the other members of the group will include you.

So You Want to Join a Writer's Group

Three Dog Night sang, "One is the loneliest number." That's how some writers feel and why they reach out to critique groups and writers' groups.

The most important questions to consider regarding critique groups are: Why do you want to join? Are you searching for a second opinion? Are you lonely? Do you want to network? Are you looking for a writing soul mate? These are all bona fide purposes for joining a group — just make sure you are clear about your needs so they can be met.

Consider these question guidelines:

- Can you take advice on your work? Can you disagree with a critique of your work without becoming hostile?

- Have you read the work of some of the writers in the group you plan to join? Is it the same or slightly above the caliber of your own work?

- Can you respect the people you'll be meeting with?

- Are you comfortable in their presence?

- Are their meetings convenient? Are they organized?

- Are the members of the group professional in their discussions of other writers' work?

- Would joining a large, national organization with monthly meetings and specific workshops be better than an intimate group?

You might want to start from scratch and create a group of your own. It takes work and enthusiasm and someone (probably you) must be in charge of the organizational requirements. A writers' group functions best if it focuses on one specialty (mysteries, romances, cookbooks, biographies), but the group can blend fiction and

nonfiction genres if everyone is willing to be helpful.6.
Use questions to host the conversation. For instance you
might ask, "You've been in publishing reference books
for some time, Margaret. How have the topics changed in
recent years?" Or, "With your comments about baby
boomers and their money fears, Ellen, do you think there
will be even more books on investments and the financial
worries of Generation X?" Ask questions that include:
who, what, why, when, where, and how. Avoid questions
that can be answered with yes or no.

7. "Here's my card." Use this sentence throughout the
   conference and ask for business cards from the people you
   meet. If you're not experienced handing out business cards,
   it may feel awkward at first — most new things do — but
   keep at it. Remember, the people you meet want to know
   how to get in touch with you. Your business card is a tool
   they will use to find you or refer you to one of their
   colleagues.

To meet as many people as possible, you need to move
gracefully around the room. There are things that are worse
than being cornered at a conference with a tedious conversational partner, but when you're the one who is stuck, you
might be hard pressed to think of anything worse. Here are
some suggestions.

1. Smile and wait for a lull in the conversation.

2. If you're in a group, you can say, "Will you excuse me.
   There's someone I've been waiting to speak with." Moving
   on to refresh your soda, get a cup of coffee, or say hello to
   an old friend are also excellent exits.

3. If there are just two of you, you might say, "After what
   we've been talking about, I know you'd enjoy meeting
   John." Move out of the conversational duo and add, "Let
   me introduce you." Then move the person over to John's
   group.

4. If you don't know anyone else in the room, suggest that you both move into another small group or join another person who is standing alone.

Remember, you want to connect with as many people as time permits. You must leave conversations to do so.

Writers' conferences are excellent places to network with other writers; however, you are there to learn. Spend time listening to the experts. Spend time listening to the concerns, hopes, and dreams of other writers. You won't feel alone. Get business cards and chat with other writers after the conference is over.

Five Minutes of Writing

Get ready to set the alarm — you're going to write the forgotten. Remember to put yourself in the picture and picture yourself in a place, with smells, feelings, and other people.

Choose one of the following and write for five minutes:

- *All families have black sheep, and in ours it is . . .*

- *After my car hit the . . .*

- *Working for an unbridled bully is . . .*

- *The true meaning of success is . . .*

Stop after five minutes. Take a break. Return to this exercise and read it out loud.

CHAPTER 12

Making Your Book Happen

All is fish that comes to the literary net.
Goethe puts his joys and sorrows into poems,
I turn my adventures into bread and butter.
— Louisa May Alcott

You've been waiting and it has *finally* happened: Your book is out. What I'm going to tell you now may not be pleasant to hear, but every published writer will say it's true. No matter how much your publisher does to publicize your book, from print advertisements to television spots, you will not consider it enough. The message here is, *you* must make your book happen. The alternative is to hire a publicist to do it for you, for a few thousand dollars a month.

In this final chapter we'll go over ways to announce your book, create your own mailing list, and get your network to help you promote your book. While working cooperatively with your publisher's PR department, you will learn to design and use publicity materials and press releases, arrange to teach workshops and give presentations, and contact book reviewers and the media. And by writing spin-off articles, you'll find out how to not only increase your income, but also extend the life and sales of your book. Note: If your book is still in the thought, proposal, or draft stage, ingest these tips. You'll need them soon.

No, the work isn't over yet. To be truthful, when the book arrives at bookstores and the copies come to your mailbox, your real work begins.

Announcing Your Book

You've struggled, you've slaved, and you've sweated through the writing and editing process. Okay, so you wouldn't have missed it for the world, but it was a lot of hard work, and now your book is out. Whether it has been published by one of the big houses or a smaller one, or it's a self-published book, this is a scary and exciting time.

If it's coming to a bookstore near you, on your mark, get set, and go! Here are some ways to promote your book:

1. **Plan to Promote.** When the book is about to be released, there's good news and bad news. It's good that you finally have a product to sell. The bad news is that you must put aside any preconceived notions of individualized publicity assistance from the publisher. It will take your energy and love for the book to make it happen. You have work to do, and the success of your book will be a direct reflection on just how hard you work to sell it. If you wait for the publisher to do it all, it won't get done to your satisfaction, regardless of who the publisher is.

2. **Connect with Reviewers.** Before your book is scheduled for release, get the name and phone number of the publisher's publicity staffer. Make friends with this person. Talk yourself up and be ready to stress the competency of your public speaking skills. The PR person should be able to tell you or find out where the publisher has sent review copies and what publicity, if any, is being done by the publisher.

Remember, it's okay for you to send a press release and a letter to reviewers asking that the book be reviewed. If you want your book to sell, you can't be shy, even if that's your normal behavior. So if you contact reviewers, what's the worst that can happen? Someone might think you're the successful, pushy type. That's a good problem.

The purpose of writing to book reviewers is to offer to send them a review copy of your book, so that they will, of course, review it. Don't just send out a form letter that looks like one. Make each letter personalized and neat. Enclose a pre-stamped postcard or SASE along with your phone number and e-mail address so that the reviewer can respond easily to your offer.

3. **Advertise, Advertise.** Ask your publisher to make up a flier about the book and send you 300 copies of it or one clean copy to photocopy. Or design one yourself. If you're a certified klutz when it comes to graphic design, network to find a designer who can do the work. You can also check out some of the very simple software programs that make you look like a brilliant advertising genius.

The advertisement — this is exactly what it is — can be a simple postcard or an 8$\frac{1}{2}$-inch by 11-inch flier printed on colored paper. Why a flier or card? You need to be able to leave it at bookstores, during promotional activities, and at the library. The flier or postcard is also great to have on hand when you do workshops or free presentations.

You may also want to have bookmarks made up, with the cover of your book on the front and how to reach you printed on the back. Call around for printing costs — they vary a lot. You can also use desktop publishing programs to produce great giveaway materials. Your giveaways might also include buttons, greeting cards, inspirational messages, doorknob hangers (much like *Do Not Disturb* signs in hotels). If you have a budget for it and a printer who can do a good job, you can recreate the cover of your book on coffee coasters, T-shirts, and canvas bags.

4. **Enlist Your Network.** Make a mailing list of everyone in your network — this includes friends, family, distant cousins, members of writers' clubs, college chums, as well as business associates and colleagues. Send this list to your PR person at the publishing house, asking to have everyone on your list sent a flier or press release. Don't be surprised if the PR person doesn't want to do this. Often, it's up to us, as authors, to do this extra work. If the publisher doesn't have the staff to help you, send the fliers yourself. Be sure to keep a record for tax purposes of how much you spend.

5. **Get Your Book into Bookstores and Libraries.** Write a short, snappy note to all those folks on your network mailing list. Write something like: "Dear family, friends, associates, colleagues, and fellow writers, I need your assistance . . . " Ask these people to take the flier to their local bookstores and libraries requesting (or demanding) that your book be added to the shelves. This really works. Ask for help from your retired relatives. They are incredible sales people; they love to hawk the books of their literary relations.

6. **Be in the Picture.** If you haven't done so before, have a professional black and white photo taken of yourself. Use it for newspapers, magazines, promotional purposes, and, we hope, television. Find a photo duplication service used by the entertainment industry (in such places as New York or Los Angeles) and have bunches of copies made. Each copy costs from 25 to 50 cents, and the more you buy the cheaper they become.

7. **Get the Word Out.** Write and send a news release to your local newspaper, your regional newspaper, cable television shows, your alumni newsletter, and the writer's magazines to which you subscribe. Tell them the news about your book; when and where you're available for interviews, articles, and quotes; and tell them what you can talk about.

Include a list of ten possible questions that they might use in interviews with you.

8. **Sign Books.** Call your local bookstores and arrange for a book signing. If your book is self-published, call local businesses that should carry your book, drop off a sample copy and arrange for a book signing. Enlist the help of twenty friends and family members, and if necessary beg, bribe, or blackmail them into showing up at the signing. Have them cluster around you and smile a lot. Have them rave about the book. Promise them cookies or whatever you need to do, so that they will come to the signing.

The more people milling around you, the more books you'll sell to strangers. People feel slightly intimidated approaching an author, but when there are others already asking questions, then the comfort level increases. Remember, a book signing is news and the local newspaper should be told.

9. **Share Your Profits.** Do some charity events and tie your book in. Donate a portion of sales of the book or sales for that day to the charity. This is news, and the charity's PR person should be able to help you get some media coverage. If the PR person doesn't know how to do that, share your knowledge and write your own press release for the newspapers.

10. **Break into Catalogues.** Any time you see a catalogue in which your book would be perfect, call the catalogue's sales department and find out the name of a contact person. Then write an irresistible letter and send a book. Catalogue sales are sensational. Think small and think big, too.

Selling to Quality Paperback Book Club could be a coup. It worked for me and my gold mine, _60-Second Shiatzu_ (Mills & Sanderson and Henry Holt Publishers). After the book had been out for two or three years, I received an advertisement from Quality Paperback Book Club, and I thought my book would be perfect for their list. When I called my publisher, the editor graciously nixed my idea. She said, "We've already tried to sell to them." I listened politely, then sent a book and press release to the club anyway.

It was about two months later that my editor called and said, "The most amazing thing happened — Quality Paperback Book Club is going to carry *60-Second Shiatzu*." Okay, perhaps the club staff people had changed their minds after their initial refusal to the publisher's form letter. But just maybe it was my personal letter asking the club to consider my book that did it. I believe it was the latter.

11. **Tie In with the Media.** Two of the publicity sources I count on are the *Radio/TV Interview Report* and *Book Marketing Update*. Sample issues of both are available for $5 by writing to: (the name of the publication), Box 1206, Lansdowne, PA 19050; or by calling toll free (800) 553-8002, ext. 408). These are designed for publicists and you can use them too. Published twice a month, *Book Marketing Update* gives names, addresses, and e-mail addresses for radio, TV, and magazine contacts. In *Radio/TV Interview Report*, you place an ad featuring a photo of yourself and what you will talk about on television and radio. I've had great luck with both, but I've worked hard to get that luck.

12. **Don't Quit.** Don't stop. Don't turn your future over to someone else. Instead, become a success as you become a marketing machine.

Why all the fuss and bother? As you've probably caught on, unless you become involved with the sales of your book, regardless of the publishing method or publisher, your book will not do as well.

It's been years since *60-Second Shiatzu* was published. But just recently I did an interview with *American Baby* magazine on stress-relieving techniques for new moms and got a nice plug for the book, which still generates royalties even after all these years. The key is to keep plugging if you really want a long, financially profitable life for your book.

I didn't have any knowledge of book publicity when I started learning these tricks. I've made some mistakes, including a few expensive ones, like thinking that the publisher should be in charge of publicity. The moral here is that if I can do it, so can you.

Helping the Publisher Promote Your Book

You can get ready to publicize and promote your book in a variety of ways, all of which can ultimately generate income for you. Here are some things to do and think about.

- Take a public speaking class or join Toastmasters International for help getting over presentation jitters. For women, learn to do your own television-style makeup. Although the top television shows have makeup artists available for guests, smaller cable programs send you on air as is.

- Take a class on preparing publicity material, or get a book on the subject.

- Get a copy of Dan Poynter's *The Self-Publishing Manual* (Para Publishing) regardless of who paid the publishing bill. Poynter's book is filled with invaluable information on getting publicity.

- Accept any and all public speaking and promotional opportunities. Depending on the circumstances, you can either ask for a speaking fee or donate your time.

- Buy some clothes appropriate for public appearances and television. Depending on your book's topic, you may want to wear a suit and scarf or tie, or a swimsuit and scuba gear. Make sure the clothes fit well and are comfortable. If you're wearing a $400 suit that makes sitting a nightmare, you're not going to come off as a polished speaker even if you know your topic well.

- Create a media kit or ask your publisher to send you several of the kits the house has prepared. See the section later in this chapter about Creating Promotional Materials.

- Make it easy to reach you. Get an answering machine and record a professional sounding message, not one with background sounds of the baby fussing and the terrier barking. Get dedicated phone lines for your computer's modem and your home office. When you talk with anyone from the publisher's office or the media, put on your best professional voice. If your household gets crazy and noisy at times, as mine does, ask the caller to hold for a moment, close your office door and then continue. Take notes during the conversation so that you can *promptly* respond to what you said you'd do.

- Be available for last-minute presentations and interviews. One of the tricks I've found to be successful is to let radio show hosts know that I enjoy being on the radio, and should they need a last-minute guest, I'm their expert. When you're being interviewed, speak slowly. Be able to instantly produce information on how people can buy your book.

- Before radio interviews, practice what you'll say, and especially repeat the name of your book enough times so that it flows easily. Prepare the advice or information you want to share. Make sure you have a glass of water and a tissue nearby (for emergencies during the radio program), and smile when you talk. America only hears your voice, so if you sound as exhausted, flustered, or irate as you might feel, that's exactly what will come across.

- Always have sales and book availability information ready. Be sure to include information about where people can buy the book. If you're selling the books in the back of the room after a presentation, coerce someone to help you or organize the session so you can do the sales yourself. Have the price of your book, including tax if appropriate, posted.

- Select book-signing opportunities with care, and demand (yes, you can do this) that the bookstore do publicity about your appearance at the store. The managers at the large chain stores are often so busy that they don't have time for these niceties unless you remind them; the owners and managers at the independent bookstores are just as busy but go out of their way to help authors.

- Ask for your publisher's help with publicity and be ready to follow the advice and to share the contacts you have. The game of publicity includes both of you.

Creating Your Mailing List

Every time you speak in front of a group or sell your own books at the back of the room after a presentation, you have the opportunity to develop a prime mailing list with attendees' and book buyers' names, and e-mail and regular mailing addresses.

What do you do with this list? Send information about upcoming book signings and events in which you're participating. Send fliers about your newest book. Let your mailing list people know when the book goes into the second printing, when you'll be on a national television show, when anything happens.

You can also use the list to advertise that you are available as a keynote speaker or an expert on your topic. You can use the list if you are selling books yourself, or selling workbooks, tapes, or other materials you've created for sales. Ask your new friends on the mailing list to share the information with others and to refer you and your book.

This works.

Creating Promotional Materials

A press kit, also called a media kit, needs to be part of your marketing plan. You can hire a PR person to create one for you — for a few thousand dollars. Or you can design your own.

Press kits are used by the media to evaluate potential guests for upcoming events. The kit should include:

1. **A cover letter.** This explains why you're sending the kit; that is, someone referred you, the media contact called, etc. Make sure the cover letter contains all the information necessary so that the media contact can get in touch with you easily.

2. **A press release.** The one- or two-page press release gives information about your book. This is double spaced and has all the information on how to contact you or your publisher at the top of the page. This is sales stuff, not great literature. Make it punchy.

3. **A one-page biography about you.** Here you'll list your credentials, academic degrees, area of expertise, and anything else that's interesting, entertaining, or noteworthy. Make sure it implies that you have experience in front of groups, you're comfortable in the spotlight (as in television and radio), and you love to speak with the media.

4. **A list of sample questions.** The producers of radio and television shows appreciate getting these questions to help the hosts target what you want to talk about.

5. **A list of show topics.** For instance, when speaking on radio and television about *For the Love of Children* (Health Communications), I can give funny quotes from celebrities on their parenting techniques. Depending on the audience, I might want to discuss how television can help with parenting skills. I can talk about what's right with families today. Never once do I read straight from my book or give material that is in the book. Each potential topic is a presentation on its own.

6. **Your book, or a sample of it.** If it isn't out yet, send a good color photocopy of the cover, or ask your publisher to

send you about 100 copies of the cover for your press kit.

7. **Copies of publicity.** Send clippings of articles about you, endorsements, and book reviews. Keep updating this part of your press kit as more reviews come in.

8. **A professional photograph of you.** It should be black and white and have your name printed on it. Don't nix your chances with television by not following through with this step. The media want to know what you look like before they book you.

Once you get the materials gathered, make up several kits and keep them ready to send to radio, television, and event producers.

Place the materials in a durable two-pocket folder. I always use blue because blue is supposed to be the color of communication. If your book is about mountain climbing, brown might work well. If you can make excellent photocopies of the cover of your book or you have extra book jackets, carefully glue the cover of your book to the front of the folder. Attach your business card to the pocket inside, and assemble the materials in an order that's most pleasing to you.

I place a book list directly behind my photo so that my name at the top of the list and my face are seen immediately when one opens the folder.

Don't overload the folder so that it looks fat and awkward. Select the most recent press materials and the best reviews.

Place it all in a padded envelope or a large photo mailer and send it first class. Producers usually prefer getting material in the mail rather than by fax, but ask what's appropriate if you're really talking to a contact. If you do send a fax, keep it to one or two pages, and then follow up with the full press kit. Toys, candy, flowers, treats, do not impress the media. Don't send a video sample of yourself on camera unless you're asked to do so.

Be sure to follow up all contacts. You'll want to wait about a week, especially if you're sending your kit across country.

When you call, have all the information ready, and be aware that you'll have to introduce yourself and your book to more than one person. Be ready to leave a clear, concise message on a machine. If you're flatly turned down, take it like a grown-up, and put your energy into another media event or program. There are lots of them out there.

After your interview or presentation, don't forget to write a thank-you note to the show's host, PR coordinator, and producer. Follow up a month or so after the event and ask to be kept on their list of available experts.

Writing Spin-Off Articles

If you've written a book and want to make more money for your book, you can do so by writing magazine articles. The companion book to this one, *The Successful Writer's Guide to Publishing Magazine Articles* (Rodgers & Nelsen) guides you through the magazine writing maze and answers all your questions.

You can promote your book and yourself by writing articles based on your book's content. However, this does not mean that you can unlawfully take material straight from your book. Check your publishing contract before you lift a portion of your book for a magazine article. You may be infringing on your own copyright and have to get your publisher's permission to use the material.

Each magazine article is like an advertisement, and if you've priced magazine ads lately, you know they are expensive. Best yet, when you write a magazine article based on your book or information related to your book's topic, you're increasing sales for your book and increasing your credibility as an expert. And the bio (the biographical paragraph) that appears at the end of the magazine article can include not only your name, but your book's title and how to get it.

In addition to all those benefits, you can make extra money by writing magazine articles based on the content of your nonfiction book. Do I have your interest? Excellent.

The practiced writer turns one article idea into many by rewriting the basic article idea and writing spin-off pieces using one facet of the article on which to base a totally different article. Magazine writers (and I recommend you think of yourself as one while promoting your book) use the bubble method we described in Chapter 6 to discover new ideas and different slants.

Not only can you do spin-offs from your book's research or material, but you can totally revamp ideas contained in your book, perhaps adding expert interviews and rewriting the material. When you rewrite, begin fresh. Go back to your notes, look at your bubble outlines, and check the Web for updated information. Listen to your tapes again. Rejuvenate the material you've already polished. Sometimes it's hard to dispose of your original golden words in order to overhaul a piece. But that's exactly what you have to do if you want to recycle previously published material.

Why the work? It's easier to write an article or revise an article that has potential than to go through the entire research and writing process all over again on a totally different topic. Half the work is done when you rewrite an article or when you take the main topic from a place in your book that is appropriate and spin off in a different direction.

The process of writing spin-offs from your book is good for your career and your checking account. It's also good writing practice, and the more you do it, the better you become.

From this minute forward, promise me you'll look at every chapter of your nonfiction book as a possibility for turning nuggets of material into eight, ten, or twenty different articles, fillers, columns, and opinion pieces.

Should you have the time and the desire to really make your book a hit, go back over your notes, interviews, and research. Then review the different types of articles described in Chapter 7 of *The Successful Writer's Guide to Publishing Magazine*

Articles (Rodgers & Nelsen). Design your articles based on various article genres and continue to market your book to a new consumer.

 ## Getting Something for (Almost) Nothing

Yes, you can get something for next to nothing. Before the advent of money, people bartered. By golly, smart writers do it too. If you need something, whether it's illustrations for a book or the use of a piece of equipment, try to barter. Your ability to write a well-thought-out sentence is valuable and may be worth a lot more than you think.

Local business people need brochures and other promotional tools. Your hairdresser, landscaper, or attorney may want to have you ghostwrite or collaborate on an article for a trade journal or popular magazine or newspaper. Your city's leading citizens need speeches for civic events. Someone must write them. Maybe you can work out an arrangement to barter for some non-governmental services; for example, your speechwriting services might be traded for something from the politicians' own private businesses or services. Need dental work? Suggest a newsletter to your dentist. Use the services of a pre-school or day care center? Suggest a monthly information sheet filled with parenting solutions. The possibilities are endless right in your own home town when you barter your services.

But I can hear some folks saying, "Well, I write books, not articles." Think again. I recently bartered editorial space for an article about writing for trade journals. It appeared in the print and electronic version of a well-known business magazine and provided great exposure for one of my books. The same thing happened when I wrote an article and bartered for placement in a parenting magazine based in San Diego.

You're the Expert

Once your book is out, it's up to you to keep the energy high. You can do this by writing articles based on your book's premise or other research, and you can do it by giving seminars and lectures. Yes, you'll have to practice your presentation and know the topic well. You have to be interesting, vivacious, energized, provocative, and entertaining. It takes work and nerve and a sense of adventure to put on seminars and lectures.

What do you get in return? More people buying your book. As we mentioned earlier, when you negotiate your book contract it is important to make sure you can buy books for resale, from your publisher, at a significant discount. Actually, publishers adore hearing that you, the author, plan to travel and speak and sell books. You are the best marketing person for your book because you have a vested interest in its success.

You can start big by joining the National Speakers Association, which can be reached at 1500 S. Priest Dr., Tempe, AZ 85281; or by telephone at (602) 968-2552; or at their website, www.nsaspeaker.org. You can begin on a smaller note by offering workshops, classes, and programs to your local high school or civic groups.

If you're serious about getting publicity for yourself and your book, be sure to read the how-to books on this topic. If you want to get your name and the title of your book out to thousands *free of charge*, create a seminar that can be put on at your local community college or university. When you make arrangements for the workshop or class, be sure the administration understands that you will be selling your book at the back of the room. Some organizations ask that you pay a small percentage of your profits to do so; others let you keep it all.

Remember, every day at every hotel and convention center in the world there are groups having meetings. A large percentage of these groups pay for expert speakers for their lunchtime or keynote addresses. They need you, as do schools, colleges, corporations, in-house seminars, resorts, cruises, and churches.

Don't fall for the Rodney Dangerfield line that you "get no respect." Often we have to move out of our comfort zone — our hometowns and small thinking — to get recognition. Always think big. And remember these words about success:

"If you think you can, you can.
And if you think you can't, you're right."
— Mary Kay Ash

"Action is the antidote to despair."
— Joan Baez

"Success is a science; if you have the right conditions,
you get the results."
— Oscar Wilde

"Life is to be lived. If you have to support yourself,
you had bloody well better find some way
that is going to be interesting. And you don't do that
by sitting around wondering about yourself."
— Katharine Hepburn

"Success? I don't believe it has any effect on me.
For one thing, I always expect it."
— W. Somerset Maugham

"It takes a lot of courage to show your dreams
to someone else."
— Erma Bombeck

"If one is lucky, a solitary fantasy can totally transform
one million realities."
— Maya Angelou

Power Words

Professional publicists and those who work in advertising have a list of power words that get the reader thinking, acting on something, or buying. You need to know these words too when you create publicity materials. Use them with caution. They are powerful, and too many in one sentence can muddy your meaning and produce the opposite effect.

you	easy	free
imagine	introducing	just
proven	go	switch
dramatically	call	built
why	success	announcing
sale	how-to	visit
what	advantage	learn
save	quick	idea
guaranteed	results	deserve
do	fast	fun
revolutionary	enjoy	latest
deserve	first	last chance
now	style	fresh
powerful	great	

Write

Write when you're thinking, dreaming, and working, even if you're only writing in your head. Continue to polish your book and then have the smarts to know when you're ready to let it go. That's hard.

If you want to share your success or tell how you overcame a literary hurdle, or if you have a question or want me to speak to your writing group, write me at Rodgers & Nelsen Publishing, Box 7001, Loveland, CO 80537-0001, or e-mail at RNPub@aol.com. I want to hear from you.

Write every day.

Appendix A

Recommended Reading List

All writers have their own lists of books about writing. These are my current favorites. Ask about my all-time favorite books next year, and I'll probably have changed some of this list.

American Directory of Writer's Guidelines, The, John C. Mutchler. Fresno, CA: Quill Driver Books, 1997.

Artist's Way, The, Julia Cameron. New York: Jeremy P. Tarcher Publishers, 1992.

Bird by Bird: Some Instructions on Writing and Life, Anne Lamott. New York: Pantheon, 1994.

Book Marketing Update Newsletter, John Kremer, Editor. Lansdowne, PA: Bradley Communications.

Complete Idiot's Guide to Creative Writing, The, Laurie E. Rozakis. New York: Alpha Books, 1997.

Courage to Write, The, Ralph Keyes. New York: Henry Holt, 1995.

Find It Fast, Robert I. Berkman. New York: Harper Perennial, latest edition.

If You're Writing, Let's Talk, Joel Saltzman. Rocklin, CA: Prima, 1997.

New Well-Tempered Sentence, The, Karen Elizabeth Gordon. Boston: Houghton Mifflin, 1993.

On Writing Well, William Zinsser. New York: Harper Perennial, 1994.

Portable Writer's Conference, The, Stephen Blake Mettee. Fresno, CA: Quill Driver Books, 1997.

Radio/TV Interview Report, John Kremer, Editor. Lansdowne, PA: Bradley Communications.

Self-Editing for Fiction Writers, Rennie Browne and Dave King. New York: Harper Perennial, 1993.

Successful Writer's Guide to Publishing Magazine Articles, The, Eva Shaw. Loveland, CO: Rodgers & Nelsen, 1998.

Wild Mind: Living the Writer's Life, Natalie Goldberg. New York: Bantam, 1990.

Writer's Handbook: 1999, The, Sylvia K. Burack, Editor. Boston: Writer, 1998.

Writer's Journey, The, Christopher Vogler. Studio City, CA: Michael Weise Productions, 1998.

Writer's Market (Current Year), Kirsten Holm, Editor. Cincinnati, OH: Writers Digest Books, 1999.

Writer's Resource Guide to Workshops, Conferences, Artist's

Colonies, and Academic Programs, David Emblidge and Barbara Zheutlin. New York: Watson-Guptell, 1997.

Writing Articles From the Heart: How to Write and Sell Your Life Experiences, Marjorie Holmes. Cincinnati, OH: Writer's Digest Books, 1993.

Writing Down the Bones, Natalie Goldberg. Boston: Shambhala Publications, 1986.

Writing Your Life, Lou Willett Stanek. New York: Avon, 1996.

Appendix B

Writers' Organizations

Every professional writer can benefit from being a member of one of the writers' organizations. Write for information and select the one that's best for you. Do a search online; many of the writers' organizations are developing websites.

This list, keep in mind, is not complete, because new organizations spring up all the time. For more writers' associations, check out the Web or refer to the *Encyclopedia of Associations*, Gale Research Company, available at most libraries.

AMERICAN MEDICAL WRITERS ASSOCIATION
9650 Rockville Pike
Bethesda, MD 20814

AMERICAN SOCIETY OF JOURNALISTS AND AUTHORS, INC.
1501 Broadway, Suite 302
New York, NY 10036

ASSOCIATED WRITING PROGRAMS
Tallwood House, Mail Stop 1E3
Fairfax, VA 22030

AUTHORS GUILD (and AUTHORS LEAGUE OF
AMERICA)
330 W. 42nd Street
New York, NY 10036

DOG WRITERS OF AMERICA, INC.
173 Union Road
Coatesville, PA 19320

GARDEN WRITERS ASSOCIATION OF AMERICA
10210 Leatherleaf Court
Manassas, VA 20111

HORROR WRITERS ASSOCIATION
P. O. Box 423
Oak Forest, IL 60452

INTERNATIONAL BLACK WRITERS
P. O. Box 1030
Chicago, IL 60690

INTERNATIONAL P.E.N. WOMEN WRITERS'
COMMITTEE
523 W. 11th St. No. 75
New York, NY 10024

INTERNATIONAL WOMEN'S WRITING GUILD
Box 810, Gracie Station
New York, NY 10028-0082

NATIONAL WRITERS ASSOCIATION
1450 S. Havana, Suite 424
Aurora, CO 80012

NATIONAL WRITERS UNION
13 Astor Place, 7th Floor
New York, NY 10003

PEN AMERICAN CENTER
568 Broadway
New York, NY 10012

PEN CENTER U.S.A. WEST
672 Lafayette Park Pl., No. 41
Los Angeles, CA 90057

SOCIETY OF CHILDREN'S BOOK WRITERS AND
ILLUSTRATORS
22736 Vanowen St., Suite 106
West Hills, CA 93107

TEXT AND ACADEMIC AUTHORS ASSOCIATION
Box 535
Orange Springs, FL 32182-0535

WESTERN WRITERS OF AMERICA, INC.
20 Cove Woods Rd.
Oyster Bay, NY 11771

WRITING ACADEMY
267 Maple St.
New Wilmington, PA 16142

Index

Page numbers in bold type indicate where definitions occur.